EMPOWER
THE INJURED

A How-To Guide for Handling
Your Own Personal Injury Claim

JONATHAN D. ROVEN

The information, ideas, and suggestions in this book are not intended to render legal advice. Before following any suggestions contained in this book, you should consult your personal attorney. Neither the author nor the publisher shall be liable or responsible for any loss or damage allegedly arising as a consequence of your use or application of any information or suggestions in this book.

This book is tailored towards personal injury claims in California. Nothing in this book is meant to be construed as legal advice or as a substitute for an attorney. Nothing in this book is a guarantee, warranty, or prediction regarding the outcome of any legal matter. Jonathan Roven is a licensed attorney in the State of California, is responsible for the content in this book, and can be reached at 844-9-INJURED. There is no creation of an attorney-client relationship arising out of this book. Keep in mind that the law constantly changes so make sure you are getting the most current information.

ISBN: 978-1-4834-8858-5 (sc)
ISBN: 978-1-4834-8857-8 (e)

Library of Congress Control Number: 2018908303

Cover photograph by Curtis Dahl.

Lulu Publishing Services rev. date: 8/15/2018

.

Acknowledgements

First, I'd like to thank my wife, Sarah, for her unconditional support, and the countless hours she listened to me talk about legal theory and concepts.

Second, I'd like to thank my mentor, partner, and father-in-law, Robert Kahn, and my amazing mother-in-law, Rebecca. Thank you for your continued guidance.

Third, I'd like to thank my parents, Alfred and Mona. I am truly grateful for their constant support and encouragement.

I dedicate this book to my children, Adam and Hannah.

CONTENTS

INTRODUCTION

I wrote this book to help people. There are many cases that I have to turn down either because the damages are too low, or my firm is thankfully too busy to take on certain cases. Therefore, I put together a lot of the tips that I gathered along the way with settling and litigating personal injury claims, and put them in this book for the benefit of people who do not have an attorney.

The knowledge that is contained in this book is mostly gained from my own experience of working in the personal injury field. Some of it was gained through research, but most of it was gained through hands-on experience of dealing with insurance companies on many personal injury claims.

This book was written so that you or a loved one can handle a personal injury claim on your own. This is a not all-inclusive guide on litigating large cases. This book is geared towards helping people with smaller claims so that they can perhaps gain a meaningful settlement without having to split fees with an attorney.

My hope in you reading this book is that you will be able to get the treatment that you need, put together a settlement demand package, and ultimately settle your personal injury claim all on your own.

Not every personal injury claim will fall under the category of this book. This book is mainly focused on individuals who sustained relatively minor injuries, such as a sore back or neck. If you sustained a serious injury and/or will need a lot of future care, then you should consider hiring a competent personal injury attorney because insurance companies are more reluctant to pay out on those claims.

However, if you were in an accident where you sustained relatively minor injuries, then this book should guide you in the right direction to secure a settlement for your injuries.

Disclaimer: This book is tailored towards personal injury claims in California. Nothing in this book is meant to be construed as legal advice or as a substitute for an attorney. Nothing in this book is a guarantee, warranty, or prediction regarding the outcome of any legal matter. Keep in mind that the law constantly changes so make sure you are getting the most current information.

CHAPTER 1

The First 100 Hours After Your Accident

The first hundred hours after the accident are crucial. A lot that happens in this time will affect your case down the line. If you follow these steps, you can help preserve your case.

Later in this book, we will go into greater detail regarding the topics discussed in this chapter. However, if you are in the first hundred hours of your accident, I provided a brief overview of the things you can do to best preserve your case.

Medical Treatment

Plain and simple, if you're injured in an accident, you should immediately seek medical care. You shouldn't underestimate the extent of your injuries and try to be tough – you should go to a medical provider and get an evaluation. Go to an emergency room or some provider as soon as possible after the accident, to get an evaluation and diagnosis of your injuries.

When a person waits to receive the treatment, the insurance company (or other side) can point out that since they waited to seek treatment, they were not very injured. Although this may not be true, insurance companies commonly employ this tactic to minimize a claim's value. Aside from helping your claim's value, you can get some kind of evaluation as to what your preliminary injuries are, and whether you can use that information down the line during the settlement process.

If after an evaluation you still feel pain or soreness, you should seek the opinion of a specialist. An orthopedic surgeon can be consulted at first, where they can properly diagnose the cause of the pain, and decide what the proper course of treatment will be for that pain. Additionally, a specialist's opinion (like an orthopedist) will likely have greater weightage than that of a general practitioner in the eyes of the insurance company.

Calling the Police

If you're involved in an automobile accident, you should consider calling the police so that they can create a police report. The police report will have weight when it comes to approaching the insurance companies, in terms of liability, to settle your claim. This does not mean that if the police report says that the other party is at fault that your case will be a "slam dunk," but it can help prove your side of the story. If you're not sure who's at fault, then proceed with caution, since the police report may turn against you. But if the liability is clear to you that the other person caused the accident (such as in a case where you were rear-ended while you were travelling safely), then calling the police to file a report will have a lower risk. It is best to get a police report that shows that you were injured and another person caused the accident.

The police can come and take down information regarding who was involved, how the accident occurred, and other identifiable information along with witness information. This will also help if the other party involved in the accident is not being cooperative with providing their information. That way, you can get their contact and insurance information (or lack thereof), in case you need to make a claim against their insurance or your own insurance.

Don't let the other driver convince you to not call the police. Oftentimes, the other party will try to befriend you and ask you to not deal with the police and insurance companies, but just to make a deal without insurance company involvement. Don't take the bait! People often agree to this, but it doesn't end well many times. It's better to have a police report on your side than not to have one at all, instead of battling against someone in court, who says they are not at fault, without you having much proof that they were.

When the police show up, you should get the police officer's name and badge number. If they are taking down information, they will often have a card that contains the information about the traffic collision report. Get that card so that you have an easier time obtaining the traffic collision report down the line. A traffic collision report is usually available a few weeks after the accident, so the officer or sheriff has time to draft the report. You can simply ask them when reports are usually ready, and then follow up with the department at that time.

If you notice that someone is acting aggressively, or appears to be intoxicated, you should inform the police. There are instances where a person can get attorney's fees if the liable driver was intoxicated during the accident.

You should also inform the officer if you are injured. If you need an ambulance, don't hesitate to get one to take you to the hospital. Worry about the expenses later—your health is most important.

See Chapter 2 on police reports for more details.

Witness Information

Getting witness statements and information can change a case from a weak "he-said she-said" case to a strong one. If there were witnesses to the accident, get their information as quickly as possible. You want to do this sooner rather than later to prevent any complications in gathering witness information in the future.

Get the contact information of the witnesses as well – their name, phone number, address, email address, and other information so you have a way of getting in touch with them in case you need to.

You can scout around the accident area and see whether people saw how the accident took place. If there are stores nearby, you can approach them and ask if people saw how the accident occurred.

Not only do you want to get the witness' contact information, but also ask them to recollect what they saw. Call them to try and track down everything they had witnessed pertaining to the accident. You can also document your conversation in the letter to them. Their recollection of events could be very helpful when it's time for you to present a settlement demand to the other party's insurance company, or your own.

It is possible that you will only have a single opportunity to get the witness statement. So, if you're not too injured, try and get immediate witness statements. Witnesses are generally flaky, so it's always better to get their statements right away.

You can approach a person and ask them how the accident happened. You can simply pull out your cell phone, press the record button, ask them to consent to being recorded, and ask them to state what happened. Something to keep in mind is that you shouldn't tell them what to say, but allow them to narrate how they saw the accident happen. So, you can simply ask them, "How did the accident happen?" Ask for as many details as possible.

You can even get a witness to write down their statement on a piece of paper. A statement doesn't have to be made on formal paper, it just has to say what the witness saw in terms of how the accident occurred and any other details they may have.

See Chapter 7 on "Gathering Your Evidence" for more information and sample witness statements.

Photographs

Take pictures, lots of pictures. You should have pictures of the accident, property damage, injuries, and witnesses. Photographs greatly help a case; they bring a case to life. In the case of a car accident, another form of proof as to the extent of damage to the car, is an invoice from the car repair shop detailing how much property damage there was to the car. However, photographs will have more of an impact than an invoice, so take pictures.

In addition to taking pictures of the damage to a vehicle, if there's some kind of debris or broken glass on the ground, take pictures of those as well. This will also show the severity of the accident and show why a person is likely to have been injured as a result of it.

You also want to take the types of photos that are going to show liability. Try and take pictures of the accident that will reflect how it occurred. If the pictures are good enough, you can use them to help put together exactly how the accident occurred.

If possible, try and find skid marks. If a person is about to get into an accident, what's the first thing they do? Slam on the brakes. This can be an indicator as to who is at fault. Perhaps the faulty person was driving too fast, perhaps someone came to a sudden stop causing the accident. This evidence can be helpful in establishing the cause of the accident.

You could take photos of the general area around the accident. This can include traffic signs, traffic lights, how traffic is going. You should also include pictures of all the accident-involved cars, taken from a good angle. You can take many pictures from many different angles as well. You should take pictures of the weather conditions and time of day of the accident as well–if it was raining or sunny, if it was night-time or daytime. This will give a better indication of any distractions that may have caused the at-fault driver to cause the accident.

If there's anything around you that was also damaged, such as a street post or tree, take a picture of that as well. Even though there might not be a damage claim for those objects against the at-fault party, it's still helpful in showing the severity of the accident and how it actually occurred.

Take pictures of the witnesses and anyone who is involved in the accident. You can even take photos of the police officers so that you will be able to identify them later if you need to. This will help down the line when you need to get witness statements and put a face to the name. This can also serve to show that people were actually present during the accident.

After the accident, you should take pictures of any injuries and their progression. Injuries may develop after the accident, so you can take pictures continuously afterward. Bruises may not always show up right after an accident, so you can wait a day or so to see whether they appear. It's important to photograph your injuries so that you have proof of how severe the injuries were.

Get the Information of All Parties Involved

If you have a smart phone, use it to take pictures of the other party's driver's license, license plate, proof of insurance, and registration. It's always helpful to compare the name on their driver's license with the name on the insurance documents and registration. You should also ask for their cell phone number and other contact information. Make sure to ask them whether all the information on the documentation provided to you is up to date.

Regarding insurance information, make sure that the insurance policy is in effect. The proof of insurance should have some dates that prove that the policy is effective, so make sure that the day of your accident falls within those dates. If the policy is not effective, you may be asking for compensation from your own uninsured/underinsured motorist policy.

Additionally, you should make sure that the vehicle is currently registered.

Surveillance Videos

Occasionally, there may be videos that document how accidents happen. If you go around to the property owners or nearby businesses, which have surveillance cameras, you can simply ask them whether they will release the video footage. They may not always release it right away, but they might later. If they still do not release the video, you can hire an attorney to file suit and issue a subpoena to obtain the video footage.

When Asked "Are You Hurt?"

This is a critical issue when a person doesn't know the extent of their injuries, and a police officer or someone there asks them, "Are you injured?" What's the correct answer to give them? If a person is feeling a slight soreness, the best answer is, "Yes." This may seem obvious, but many times people want to appear tough and end up saying, "I'm fine," or something of the like, which gives room to the other side to dispute whether the victim was actually injured in the accident.

If a person is not feeling injured, the correct answer is "I don't know." Oftentimes, whiplash symptoms do not appear for a few days. Therefore, a person truthfully does not know whether they are injured.

It's not a good idea to say "No" when you really are hurt, or if you don't know whether you are hurt. This happens too often and it ends up hurting a person's personal injury case.

Don't Admit to Wrongdoing

"I am so sorry!" These words should not leave your lips following an accident. It's important to refrain from making statements that will show that you are liable. For instance, you don't want to walk around saying "It's all my fault!," or "I'm so sorry." Any type of statement like this will probably get reported to the police or the insurance companies, and they will try to pin the fault on you, using this as you admitting to being liable. The best thing to do is to say as little as possible to the other drivers or passengers.

A time may come when another driver or passenger will try to get you to admit liability. They may say, "Can you sign a statement saying that you're liable?" Don't agree to anything of this sort.

It's important for a person to not automatically admit wrongdoing when they've been in an accident. The truth of the matter is that many times a person truly doesn't know whether or not they were the cause of the accident. In a case where a person rear-ends another party, the person in front could have, out of nowhere, come to a sudden stop, causing the person behind them to crash into them. The best thing a person can do is not to admit wrongdoing.

However, if the other side makes statements like that, definitely take note of it. These types of statements can help your claim.

Don't Lose Your Temper

Losing your temper can hurt your case, badly. Losing your temper can turn a great case into a terrible one, because you will turn yourself into a terrible witness. If a police officer is dealing with a person who has lost their temper, the police officer is not going to be inclined to try and help them. The police officer may even comment on a person's behavior in their report, which can negatively impact the case.

After an accident, if you can, just stay calm. If you're able to remain composed, it will likely help your case down the road. Instead, you should focus on getting the medical treatment you need right away. Let the other people involved in the accident act crazy, not you. You need to focus on the most important person involved in the accident: YOU.

Keep Track of Expenses

After the accident, you may start racking up expenses, such as travel expenses and medical bills. Keep track of all of these. You may need to take a taxi to get from one place to another, rent a car, get a new set of glasses, buy crutches, and so on. Keep your receipts so that you can ask for these expenses to be reimbursed when you are ready to settle.

Notify Your Employer

If you are going to need time off work to recuperate, let your employer know. This will help you establish lost wages when it's time to settle the case. When a doctor informs you about how long you are going to need to be off work, inform your employer.

Keep a Journal

Note down the details of your injuries and the accident. If your pain changes, for better or for worse, mark it down in a journal so that you remember it later. This can benefit your settlement because it will aid in recalling a lot of the details.

Don't Settle Right Away!

In the initial hundred hours of your case, the insurance adjuster for the other side may try to convince you to make a quick settlement. Don't fall for this. You probably don't know how injured you actually are or what the other side's maximum offer is. It is best to wait and figure out how injured you are, get the proper treatment, and not be quick to settle. If the insurance company is eager to settle right away (such as if they call and want to meet with you or give you an offer), they can probably offer you more money in the future.

Don't Post Anything on the Internet

This may be tempting for people involved with social media, but this is most likely not going to help your case. Posting a video of the accident along with a long statement about yourself is probably going to fall right into the insurance adjusters' hands. Right after an accident, a person might not feel the full effects of the accident, so they may post something online saying, "Thankfully I wasn't hurt!," or something along those lines. Insurance adjusters will love something like this because it severely damages a person's injury claim. It's better to not post anything online.

Don't Talk About Your Case

Unless it is to your doctor or your attorney (if you have one), don't talk about your case. Any statements you make to people (if they are not "privileged" communications) can be asked about later.

If Your Injuries Are Severe, You May Want to Seek a Lawyer

If you are severely injured, you may want to seek professional help. If you suffered broken bones, are going to need surgery, or are going to need treatment for months or years, then you may want to seek counsel. Your case may e a bit more complicated to resolve, and insurance companies are not likely to easily settle with you.

Chapter Summary

Here are the most important points from the chapter:

1. Seek medical attention right away.
2. Take pictures of the accident and injuries.
3. Get the contact information of everyone involved.

CHAPTER 2

Police Report

What is a police report?

A police report (or sometimes called a "traffic collision report") is a document that is drawn up by the police, sheriffs, or other personnel, which states certain aspects of a car accident. The police report in a personal injury case could be a very significant piece of evidence that can help or hurt a case. The police report will usually document each party's and witness' statements, apart from the officer's, about how the accident occurred and what its aftermath was. It will also take down the contact information of each witness, a summary of how the accident occurred, and the officer's suggestion as to who is at fault for the accident.

Dealing With an Unfavorable Police Report

Sometimes, the police report comes out unfavorably, putting you or the injured person at fault. This does not necessarily mean that the case is over; it just means that the police report is unfavorable.

Many people despair at this stage because they believe that there is no way to overcome a negative police report. But it is important to keep in mind that a police report can be disproved. We will discuss the few ways through which a report can be disproved and even altered. There are many ways to get around an unfavorable police report, which is normally dealt with at the settlement or litigation stages.

When dealing with an unfavorable police report, consider the following:

1. Was the officer an eyewitness? The officer was most likely not present when the accident occurred, and therefore didn't see how it occurred themselves. Usually, the officer comes to the accident scene some time after the accident, and gets statements from the witnesses, and therefore, has no "personal knowledge" of how the accident took place. This is an important fact to point out when making your demand or another appropriate forum (such as court or arbitration, which will be discussed later). You can emphasize that the officer or authority really doesn't "know" what happened, since they were not there and could not have possibly seen the accident.

2. Changing the police report. Some police or sheriff's departments allow for amendments (changes) or even a supplement (additions) to the police report.

Amendments are hard to obtain when they involve the faulty person. When they involve relatively minor details like the color of a car or correcting the driver's license number, amendments should be easier to obtain. However, getting an officer to change their mind is not an easy task. You can call the department that wrote the report and ask them what steps you need to take to amend the police report.

You can even call the police officer right after the accident. Generally, the police are not going to want to get involved in a dispute regarding who caused the accident, but it's worth a try. You can discuss with the officer the circumstances surrounding the accident, and let them know that you are going to try and handle this accident with the insurance company. Be sure to not tell the officer what to do regarding putting the other side at fault; that will most likely hurt your case. However, you can try to reiterate how the accident occurred, in hopes that they will see the accident from your perspective and put the other side at fault.

When speaking to the police officer, you should document what they said. This can later be helpful in the case if you need to call them as a witness, or if they have told you one thing and have written something different in their report (if they put you at fault when you shouldn't be).

A supplement can be accomplished by going down to the department and writing a statement as to how the accident occurred. You can write down your own account as to what happened. This will be helpful right after an accident because you can refer to this document to remind you of certain details, which you may forget down the line. Sometimes, months (or years) will pass before a case settles or goes to trial, and memories do not last forever. Writing a supplement of your own account will be helpful to recall many aspects of the case, which you would otherwise not remember. The effectiveness of making a supplement can somewhat be limited, when changing the minds of the insurance adjuster or the judge, because you are essentially making a favorable statement to try and sway the officer's or sheriff's opinion regarding the accident, when you have had some time to think about the accident. To supplement the police report, contact the local department and ask them what their procedure is, as each department may have their own set of procedures.

Remember, if the police report does come out unfavorably, there is no need to despair. This is just a negative aspect of the case that needs to be dealt with at the time of settlement and/or at litigation.

3. Hiring a traffic accident expert. Another way through which you can overcome an unfavorable police report is to hire an expert who will say that the police report, regarding how the accident occurred, is inaccurate. Traffic accident experts are often highly trained in the sciences such as physics. They will speak to the witnesses, look at the evidence, and do research to learn as much as they can about the accident. Then, they can "recreate" the accident to determine how the accident occurred and who is at fault. Dealing with experts is a tricky matter, but it could be vital in overcoming an unfavorable police report. The traffic accident expert can then either testify for you at trial or arbitration, or you can submit their report to the insurance company when making your demand. However, traffic accident experts can be pricey, so make sure they are worth the money.

If you do not have the money for a traffic accident expert and your injury is severe enough, consider hiring a lawyer. They may have the funds to pay for an expert so you can have a better chance at overcoming the other side putting the fault on you partially because of the police report.

Contents of the Police Report

Most traffic collision reports are written within a few weeks following the accident. Usually, when dealing with a police report, we are dealing with a car accident. However, police reports can be drawn up for other accidents as well, and their contents may be similar. You can obtain your copy of the police report within a relatively short period.

- Date, Time, and Location. The report should contain the date, time, and location of the accident. By establishing these facts, we can also determine the weather conditions. Those pieces of evidence may affect the analysis of how the accident occurred. Perhaps it was raining and the roads were slippery, or it was foggy and hard to see the car ahead. All these factors can affect the outcome of both the police report and the case.

- Identification of People Involved. This part of the report typically includes the background information of every person actually involved in the accident. It will include information like their driver's license number, name, address, phone number, and so on.

- Insurance Information. The report will also likely include all drivers' insurance policy numbers. This information is critical in cases where a person forgets to obtain the other driver's insurance information and identification. What will not be included is each driver's coverage amount. That information, if needed, will have to be obtained later.

- Officer Identification. There will, most likely, be a part of the report that identifies the officer or sheriff who prepared the report. This may be helpful later if you want to contact that authority and use them as a witness at trial.

- Background Information of the Accident. Some reports will have a section that gives a lot of background information, such as the weather, lighting, roadway service, cell phone use, pedestrians involved, etc. This is helpful in determining not just who is at fault, but other factors as to why they are at fault. Or, if the police report is unfavorable, these factors can be used to show that the police report is contradictory and not a good representation of who is at fault.

- Witnesses. Witnesses are especially important to a case because generally they are the "uninterested parties," which means they usually don't have a stake in the case. The reason they are important to a case is because their testimony can be seen as more credible, since they have nothing to gain by telling their story. Whereas, the victim and the other people involved do have something to lose, whether it be money, a point on their record, insurance premiums going up, or other factors. Witnesses may not have those interests and therefore, their testimony carries a lot of weight.

- Statements. The officer may take statements from the witnesses and write them down in their report. This is a good indication of what a witness will say later, if you need them to testify on your behalf. Also, if they try to turn their story against what they said in the police report, you can note that as well, if it is unfavorable to your side of the story.

- Summary and Cause of Accident. This part of the report helps or hurts a case the most. Who does the officer or sheriff believe is at fault? This part of the report should identify that information.

What If There Is No Police Report?

Police reports are not vital to a case. Many cases can proceed without ever having a police report. You can prove your case without a police report through many different methods. You can use witness testimony, based on eyewitness accounts as to what occurred at the accident. You can use a traffic analysis expert to state how the accident occurred. And simply enough, you can use your own testimony.

Other things to look for, if you don't have a police report, are perhaps surveillance cameras in the area, traffic cameras, and cell phone pictures. Visit Chapter 7 on "Gathering Your Evidence" to find out more information on the types of evidence that you can obtain to help prove your case, even without a police report.

How to Obtain a Copy of the Police Report

To obtain a copy of the police report, you will need to know the police, sheriff's, or other government department who wrote the report. Then, you can either search online to find the information and fees, which they need to process your request, or you can directly call the department and ask them what form to fill out, information to provide, and the fee needed. Each department may have their own set of rules. One may require notarized documents, another may not, and their fees may differ.

CHAPTER 3

Determining Liability: Negligence

The most common type of liability for personal injury is negligence. Negligence is defined as a person failing to act reasonably, which results in an injury to another. For example, a driver of a vehicle is speeding down a residential street (failing to act reasonably), and rear-ends into the back of a vehicle, causing the driver of that vehicle injuries.

To prove negligence, you would have to prove that the person who caused the accident failed to act reasonably, and that their failure to act reasonably caused the accident, resulting in damages (such as an injury, lost wages, and pain and suffering). In car accident cases, we need to prove the following:

1. The at-fault party caused the car accident;
2. The car accident caused your injuries; and
3. What your injuries are (this is discussed in detail in Chapter 8: Compensation for an Injury Claim)

The At-Fault Party Negligently Caused the Accident

To prove that a person negligently caused the accident, we need to show that they had a duty to act reasonably, failed to do so, and that failure caused the accident. A duty to act reasonably essentially means that a person needs to act reasonably given the circumstances. For example, if you're driving a car, you need to drive it with reasonable care. A person who's driving 75 miles per hour down residential streets is not exercising reasonable a duty of care. A person who is looking at their phone while driving is also not exercising a reasonable duty of care. In many instances, a person might be driving at an unsafe speed, may not be looking at the road, might fail to yield when someone is making a turn, and so on. These are general examples of many car accident cases.

How can you use this information to your advantage?

If there is a police report following the accident that places the other party at fault, the report usually contains a portion about who caused the accident and why. You can simply use that part of the police report and copy it into your demand letter to show that the at-fault party negligently caused the accident.

If there is no police report, then you will need to specifically state how the driver negligently caused the accident. More of this will be discussed in detail in Chapter 10: How to Write a Demand Letter.

Negligence Presumption

There are certain situations where a person is "presumed" or already believed to be negligent by the court, and it is up to them to prove that they are not negligent. This is an incredibly useful tool because the other side is already facing liability, which would put you in a highly leveraged position to try and settle your case. This is generally referred to as "negligence per se."

To be liable under negligence per se, a person must have violated a specific law, and the violation was a "substantial factor" in causing harm. How do we know what law they violated? As stated before, many times in the police report, the officer will write down the exact code section that a person has violated. You can quote that portion of the police report in your demand to the insurance company, and that should help in getting you the settlement you deserve. In your demand letter, you can write something like, "Liability in this case is clear as your insured violated the Vehicle Code as the officer cited in the police report."

Negligence per se is not always going to apply to your situation. The other side's insurance company can simply respond to you saying they are not liable under that code section. Many times, in he-said she-said cases (where there are no witnesses or documents proving the other side at fault, and it is the word of each party involved against the other's), the insurance company will have an easier time denying liability, even if the police report says their insured (the person they are insuring) violated a certain law, causing the accident.

Also, there are many exceptions to negligence per se, like if the violation of the law was reasonable or necessary in a certain circumstance. For example, you may argue that a person was driving too fast which caused the accident, but what if someone else was about to side-swipe them? Yes, they may have been speeding, but it was to avoid an accident caused by someone else, and in doing so, caused an accident with you. That may absolve or relinquish a person's liability under negligence per se.

Parents Liable for Child's Negligence

In short, parents or guardians can be held "jointly" liable for any accidents the minor causes. The parent is potentially liable for all foreseeable damages, if they permitted the child to drive the car. Therefore, if you are injured because of a child's negligence, you can report it to the parents' insurance company and seek recovery.

Hit by An Emergency Vehicle

If an emergency vehicle, such as an ambulance or fire truck, is responding to an emergency, with their sirens on and the red lights flashing, and hits you or your car, they may not be liable. This is not a clear-cut rule, because you can still argue that the driver did not use reasonable care when acting in the emergency situation, to try and obtain some coverage from the employer. If you are hit by a government employee, keep in mind that the statute of limitations (deadline to act) for personal injury is much shorter than usual. It is typically six months from the date of injury, subject to exceptions. See Chapter 6 on Statute of Limitations. It is generally not recommended to sue the government without the assistance of an attorney since the rules are complicated and can include pre-filing procedure where a person can run the risk of ruining their case.

Employer's Liability

Generally speaking, an employer is responsible for the damages caused by the negligent conduct of their employees if they are acting on the job. In legal jargon, this is called "respondeat superior" or "vicarious liability." If the other person is acting during the course and scope of their employment, you may be able to seek compensation from their employer.

However, it is not a simple question as to whether a person was on-the-job when the accident occurred. This is a legal question that would either need to be argued and accepted by the employer's insurance company, or would have to be taken to court. To argue that the person who caused the accident was acting in the scope of employment, you should show either (1) that the employee's conduct was related to the tasks that they are hired to do, or (2) the employee's conduct was foreseeable given their employment responsibilities.

An example of where an employer would likely be liable for an employee's negligence in a car accident is as follows: If a driver for a delivery service causes an accident while they are on duty, then the employer would likely be liable for that accident.

In this kind of situation, you can put the other driver's employer's insurance company on notice that you were in an accident, that it was during the course and scope of the employee's employment, and that you are seeking medical treatment. At that point, you should be able to go after their insurance for coverage. A person may want to go after an employer's insurance because they may have a bigger policy and not be limited to the other driver's smaller policy.

More Than One Person At Fault – Apportionment of Responsibility

If more than one person causes the accident, there is still liability to those who caused the accident. If two people caused the accident, then they both may be liable for the damages.

In California, you can recover from the person who caused the accident by their percentage of fault. So if two people caused the accident, resulting in someone's injuries, then they each may have to pay half of the compensation owed to the victim.

Your Own Fault – Comparative Fault

The other side or their insurance may say that you were partially at fault and that your negligence was a substantial factor in causing you harm. An example of comparative fault is as follows: Let's say Simon is speeding down a residential street and Rubin runs out into the street without looking. Simon was negligent for driving unsafely, and Rubin was negligent for running out into the street without looking. Therefore, the liability may be split between the parties. If Simon is held 50% liable, then Rubin may only recover 50% of his damages from Simon.

If the insurance company is placing blame on you, then they may only be willing to pay the percentage of the money that they believe you are entitled to. This problem is two-fold (at least). First, their calculation of the money that you are owed may be low. Second, the percentage of blame that they are placing on you may be excessively high. For example, you may value your case at $20,000 and accept 25% fault, so you would walk away with $15,000. The insurance company may value your case at $10,000 and place 75% blame on you, so you would walk away with $25,000.

This happens very often in car accident cases. Insurance companies will often try to place partial blame on you. Why? Because it saves them money. There are at least two ways to overcome this. First, you should address this issue in your demand letter or other letter with the insurance company. This is discussed in more detail in Chapter 10: How to Write a Demand Letter. Second, you should address this in court, if your case gets there. This is discussed in more detail in Chapter 15: Evidentiary Hearings.

CHAPTER 4

Insurance

Insurance is a rather broad topic, but crucial to understanding how a persona injury claim works. Whether a person has insurance will weigh heavily on whether an attorney takes a case and how likely the victim will recover monetarily.

Are They Insured?

Generally, it is much more difficult to collect money from an individual than it is from insurance companies. Individuals place an emotional importance on parting with their money. On the flipside, the insurance company sees paying a settlement as an emotionless business decision. Generally, in personal injury matters, you are better off dealing with an insurance company than with an individual person.

Put the Other Side's Insurance on Notice

When a person gets into an accident, they should put the other side's insurance company on notice that they were injured in an accident and request the policy limits (how much money there is available for the accident). This does not mean that they should submit to a recorded statement from the other side's insurance company, but simply put them on notice. Here is an example of a notice letter:

"VIA FIRST CLASS MAIL

June 1, 20XX

Insurance Company
123 Coverage Lane
Insured, MI 12345

To Whom It May Concern:
   Please be advised that I was injured in an accident on MM/DD/YYYY with your insured. I am currently seeking medical treatment because I was injured as a result of the incident. I am requesting that your insured disclose the policy limits.

Sincerely,
Iman Pain"

Other Side's Insurance Coverage – Bodily Injury

If the other side's insurance company deems their own insured at fault, then they may pay you a portion or all of their coverage. This enables you to recover as much as the coverage amount, known as the "policy limit." So, if you are injured in an accident, and the other side has a limit of $15,000 per person and $30,000 per accident for Bodily Injury Coverage, then the maximum amount you can recover is $15,000 (subject to rare exceptions). If there are two or more people that were injured by the at-fault party (aside from himself), then the maximum that is recoverable is $30,000. This can become a problem if there are many people who are injured in the same accident, all needing treatment, but the policy limit of $30,000 is to be divided amongst them.

   The policy limit is an important figure regarding your case and is used to properly evaluate how much treatment you may want to get. If the other side has a limit of $15,000 for bodily injury coverage, you may think twice about getting surgery costing $20,000, which you may be on the hook for down the line.

This is not meant to overwhelm the reader. This is meant to make the injured person simply understand that if they are going to need serious treatment, they should seek legal counsel to help with the situation. There are going to be situations where the injury is severe enough that it would be better to have a professional handle the situation. This book is meant for smaller claims where injuries are not as severe, such as in cases with back and neck soreness. However, should someone require more serious treatment, like surgery, then they should consider hiring a lawyer.

How to Find Out the Other Side's Policy Limit

The policy limit may be requested in a simple letter to the adjuster. Unfortunately, the adjuster or the insured (person who is covered under the insurance) may not release that information. Should that be the situation, the alternative way to obtain the policy limit is to proceed to litigation and request that information as a part of a lawsuit. If you are approaching a situation where you need to know the policy limits as your medical expenses are escalating, then you may want to seek legal counsel to help manage the situation.

Here is a sample letter that you can send to the claim adjuster requesting the policy limits:

"VIA FIRST CLASS MAIL

June 1, 20XX

Adjuster
Fair Insurance Company
123 Happy Lane
Pleasantville, CA 91112

Claim #:   000456789-1
Your Insured: Yura T. Fault
Injured: Iman Pain
Loss Date: June 1, 20XX

DEMAND LETTER

Dear Adjuster:

It is hereby requested that the policy limits be disclosed in the above-referenced matter.

Sincerely,
Iman Pain"

When the Other Side's Coverage is Too Low in Car Accidents

There are many situations where the other side's insurance company's policy is simply not enough to cover your medical bills, pain and suffering, and lost wages. What can you do in this situation? After getting the other side's insurance to "tender the policy" (paying you the entire policy amount pertaining to the coverage), you can check your own insurance policy to see whether you have uninsured/underinsured motorist (UM/UIM) coverage to pay you more.

To find out how much coverage you have, look at your Declarations Page that your insurance company should have provided you, which will show your coverage amounts pertaining to the accident, or you can call your insurance company and ask them what your uninsured/ underinsured motorist policy is.

The UM/UIM coverage works like this: If the other side does not have enough insurance to cover your claim, then you request *your own insurance pay for the remainder of the claim.* You can demand your own insurance to pay you what the other insurance company did not pay you, up to a certain limit. I will explain this more below.

When the Other Side Paid Their Policy Limit But You Want More From Your Own Insurance

The UM/UIM coverage amount does not necessarily mean that you are able to ask for the amount in its entirety. The insurance company is entitled to an "offset," meaning that the former insurance policy gets reduced against the persons on a UIM policy. Here is an example:

Rubin gets into a car accident. Rubin racks up $20,000 in medical bills. The other side's insurance company has a $15,000 policy limit. Rubin has a $25,000 Underinsured Motorist (UM) policy limit. Rubin settles with the other side's insurance for the $15,000 policy limit. The maximum that Rubin can get against his own UIM policy is $10,000 because his own insurance company is entitled to an offset of $15,000 ($25,000 − $15,000 = $10,000). Rubin ends up walking away with $25,000; $15,000 from the first insurance company, then $10,000 from his own insurance company.

When pursuing your own insurance company for compensation in an accident case, you will essentially follow the same procedures as outlined in this book as you would against the other driver. The main difference is that your own insurance company may force you to go to arbitration instead of small claims court, as will be discussed in later chapters 14 and 15. Don't be surprised when your own insurance company seems less friendly to you than they were when you first obtained the policy!

If you already settled with the other side's insurance company and you want to pursue a claim against your own underinsured motorist policy, you can send your own insurance company a letter like this:

"VIA FIRST CLASS MAIL

June 1, 20XX

Happy Insurance Company
456 UM/UIM Drive
Insured, MI 12345

To Whom It May Concern:
I have settled my case with the third party for the policy limits of $15,000 for the injuries I sustained at the accident, which took place on MM/DD/YYYY. Enclosed are the documents pertaining to the settlement. I am now pursuing an Underinsured Motorist Policy claim against Happy Insurance Company. Please send me all documents that you require with regard to an Underinsured Motorist claim.

Sincerely,
Iman Pain

Enclosed: Settlement Documentation"

Important: If a pedestrian is hit by a car, the pedestrian can seek coverage from their own UM/UIM policy even though they were not in a car.

When the Other Side's Coverage Does Not Exist, or is Unknown in Car Accidents

When the other side does not have coverage, or their identity is unknown (such as in a hit and run), then you can seek coverage from your own uninsured motorist (UM) policy. This typically occurs in hit-and-run accidents or if the other driver's auto insurance has lapsed.

In this situation, you can put your own insurance on notice of the accident, and start the process with your own insurance company in a similar manner as you would if you were dealing with another insurance company.

Once you find out that the other side's identity is unknown or they don't have insurance, you can send your own insurance company a letter like this:

"VIA FIRST CLASS MAIL

June 1, 20XX

Happy Insurance Company
456 UM/UIM Drive
Insured, MI 12345

To Whom It May Concern:
On MM/DD/YYYY, I was involved in an accident and sustained injuries. I am currently seeking treatment. The other driver [indicated that they do not have insurance, and that was confirmed in the police report] or [is unknown as they simply drove off after hitting] or [insert

reason why other driver is unknown or how you believe they do not have insurance]. I am now pursuing an Uninsured Motorist Policy claim against Happy Insurance Company. Please send me all documents that you require with regard to an Uninsured Motorist claim.

Sincerely,
Iman Pain"

Medical Payments Coverage

Medical payments coverage (med pay) can pay for your treatment regardless of who is at fault. If you have this type of coverage and are in an accident, you can still get treatment for your injuries before fault is found and have your insurance company pay for it. This means that if you are injured in an accident, you can immediately see a doctor or medical provider and give them your insurance information so that the insurance company can be billed directly. The treatment coverage is up to a certain point. You can find out your coverage by checking your insurance coverage declarations page or calling your insurance company. Medical payments coverage can also cover passengers.

If the other side is deemed at fault, your insurance company can seek reimbursement for the amount they paid out for medical payments coverage from the other side's insurance company. However, generally you will be left out of this dispute.

Preventive Tip: When seeking medical payments coverage, you should also evaluate your health insurance. If you have really great health insurance where you are not going to be out of pocket for medical expenses, then medical payments coverage may be unnecessary. It is probably better to have medical payments coverage and be on the safer side. Even if it is going to be difficult to request compensation based on your injury if you are at fault, at least you can get treatment.

Medical payments coverage does not cover all types of medical treatment. The treatment must be reasonable and necessary, must be used to treat the injuries from the accident, and should be accepted treatment in the medical community. To be more familiar with this, you should know what exclusions the medical payments coverage does not cover. You can either 1) read the policy, 2) ask your adjuster or 3) contact a personal injury attorney and ask.

Property Damage Coverage

This type of coverage will typically cover personal property loss in an accident, such as your car. Property damage coverage will also have its own policy limit, which will be separate from a bodily injury policy.

Oftentimes, you may be dealing with a "property damage adjuster" who is separate from the "bodily injury adjuster." Don't be surprised if you are speaking with several people regarding one accident.

What If You Didn't Have Auto Insurance At the Time of the Accident?

If a person is injured in a multi-car collision in California, and does not have insurance, they will likely not be able to get compensation for pain and suffering. This is referred to as Proposition 213. This is a rather unfortunate chain of events because if a person is not at fault, they will not be able to recover for their pain and suffering, no matter how severe. So suppose a person gets into a car accident and will be experiencing pain for the rest of their life. How much can they recover for their pain? Zero.

However, Proposition 213 is not applicable in all situations. Some situations where Proposition 213 may not apply are when you were the passenger in an automobile accident, or if the vehicle you were driving was insured, or if you were a pedestrian.

If a person's accident is governed by Proposition 213, then they can only recover "economic damages" such as medical expenses and lost wages.

Double check your automobile insurance to make sure it does not lapse.

CHAPTER 5

When to Communicate With the Other Side's Insurance Company

A person should be very careful when being in contact with the other side's insurance company. They should realize that the insurance company has one goal in mind: to minimize the amount of the claim. Insurance companies want to pay out as little money as possible, so they have devised very clever and useful strategies to minimize your claim and the claim of anyone who was injured in an accident.

Since you are likely representing yourself, you will inevitably need to speak to the other side's insurance company (assuming you have their information and they are insured) when you want to start demanding a settlement.

Don't Give a Recorded Statement Unless It's Necessary

People will generally give information that is going to harm their case in the recorded statement. Adjusters are well equipped to asking questions in specific ways to reduce their insured's liability and try to put liability on you. If the other side's insurance company asks the injured to give a recorded statement, they can simply say something like, "I prefer not to give a recorded statement at this time."

In larger cases, you should consider not giving a recorded statement and instead hire an attorney. Larger cases include those where there are serious injuries requiring surgery, life-long ailments, or long-term treatments, or even the death of a loved one. In these types of cases, a recorded statement prior to a lawsuit will likely hurt your case. A competent attorney should prepare you for a statement in a formal setting (such as a deposition or trial).

However, in smaller cases where filing suit might not be worth the trouble (don't let the insurance company know you are considering not filing a lawsuit), you may want to give a recorded statement to get a settlement offer from the insurance company. But if possible, you may want to have an attorney listening in on the call, so that way they can try and prevent you from saying something that may hurt your case.

Right After the Accident

The best-case scenario is to not be in contact with the other side's insurance company immediately after the accident. In many instances, especially whiplash cases, a person might not yet know the true extent of their injuries. What often happens is that the other side's insurance company will be in contact with the injured at this point, when they have not fully assessed how injured they actually are (since feeling the symptoms of whiplash often takes a few days), and the injured will say that they are not so injured when they really are because they have not yet felt their symptoms. This could be very damaging to the case down later on. The solution here is that the person should not give a recorded statement right away, and not without counsel. However, if they do decide to give the insurance company a recorded statement, they should first find out the true extent of their injuries. They should seek a medical professional's opinion to find out the extent of their injuries.

Even if the other side's insurance company calls over and over again, you are not obliged to talk to them yet. You can still get a diagnosis for your injuries and then reach out to them when you want to start the settlement process. Don't be intimidated to contact them back right away, even if they leave multiple messages. Simply get your treatment and contact them when the time is right. Obviously, if there is an important deadline coming up (such as the statute of limitations), then you should contact them to attempt to settle your claim, or file the appropriate documents to preserve your claim so that you do not waive your right to recovery (see Chapter 6 on Statute of Limitations).

If you are representing yourself, then the insurance adjuster will likely call you. What sometimes happens is that a person will pick up and chat with the adjuster on a regular basis, significantly hurting their case each time they speak. For example, the adjuster may reach out regularly to check how the injured is feeling, asking if they feel any better, and the injured person may respond with something like, "I'm feeling much better!" These kinds of statements can reduce their case's value. It is better to speak with the insurance adjuster as little as possible about your injuries, only to the extent necessary to resolve your case. It doesn't matter how nice they are, they are not your friend.

The Purpose of the Recorded Statement

The adjuster wants to get your version of what happened in the accident. Some adjusters simply want to understand the bigger picture regarding what happened after reviewing records, talking to witnesses, and talking to the parties involved. However, recorded statements are usually taken to trick you into making statements that make you seem more at fault, or that their client is not at fault. You can always refuse the recorded statement, however, the insurance company may request that you submit to one prior to them giving a settlement offer. This means that you will either have to submit to a recorded statement or proceed to litigation.

Seeking Medical Attention

It is critical that a person seeks medical attention after an accident before being in contact with the other side's insurance company. Even if they feel a slight soreness, that soreness can develop into an actual injury that will require treatment, whether it's physical therapy or something more aggressive. That way, when the other side's insurance company contacts you, you can tell them that you have sought medical treatment, and you can let them know what your diagnosis is. This will likely add value to your case.

The longer a person delays, and the more time that goes by between the accident and seeking medical treatment, the more likely the other side's insurance company will say something like, "Well, you could not have been that injured if you took so long to see a medical professional." This happens quite often in personal injury cases and attorneys refer to it as "gaps in treatment." This damages the case. The best solution is to seek medical treatment and get a proper diagnosis shortly after an accident.

The Recorded Statement

A recorded statement involves the insurance company recording you talking about how the accident occurred, how you're feeling, whether you were injured, whether you went to see a doctor, and other questions that may seem irrelevant. The recorded statement usually lasts about 15-20 minutes.

We don't usually recommend that a client sit for a recorded statement, especially in a larger case, one where the client is more severely injured. If a person is going to give a recorded statement, then obviously follow the tips listed. A person may not be feeling the effects of their injuries right away, and they may minimize their injuries to the adjuster in a prematurely recorded statement. If it is your own insurance company requesting the statement, then you should cooperate with them and give the recorded statement. It is very important that you cooperate with your own insurance company, as not cooperating with your own insurance could result in a denial of coverage. However, giving a recorded statement to the other side's insurance company right away is usually not recommended.

The recorded statement is designed to negatively impact your case. The insurance adjusters are trained to ask questions in certain ways to try and minimize your claim. They will try and ask you questions in ways that are difficult to answer, so they can point out inconsistencies later in your story.

Here are some tips, should you choose to give a recorded statement:

1. Be Honest. You should only speak truthfully. The insurance company wants you to lie during your recorded statement,

that way they can pin you down as not being credible, and pay you less on that basis. Your honesty regarding the accident can maintain your case's value. By being untruthful, you are putting your case at risk of losing value.

2. **Don't Offer More Information Than You Need To.** During the questions, you should simply answer the questions that are being asked. For example, if asked, "Did you have any passengers?" an appropriate response would be "Yes," or "No." An inappropriate response would be something like, "Yes I was driving because I was leaving my ex's house who just broke up with me, and I was so distraught I could barely think about what I was doing," or "This is the worst timing because I just got laid off." Offering more information is potentially harmful to your case. Don't give a story, just answer the questions.

    The adjuster wants you to give more information so that they can try to devalue your claim. They are usually great listeners because the more information they know, the more it can hurt you. Don't think they are being polite by being silent while you speak, they are simply looking to minimize your claim.

3. **Don't Exaggerate.** You may want to say how badly you are hurt, or how negligent the other side was, but you should be careful not to over-exaggerate as that may hurt your case. During the recorded statement the insurance company might ask, "On a scale of 1 to 10, how are you feeling?" This is a rather vague question, but it would be appropriate to answer between the 7 to 8 range, if a person does have significant soreness, that way the injured doesn't downplay their own injuries. If you answer "10" and you are feeling slight soreness, then this can be pointed out later and be used against you, saying that you are not being honest with your answers. A "10" generally means intolerable pain. It is better to be honest and not exaggerate.

4. **Listen to the Question Being Asked.** Insurance adjusters are skilled at asking questions in certain ways to get answers, which

are going to hurt your case. They may seem overly friendly, but they are not. The adjuster may make a comment about your injuries, and you should carefully respond rather than trying to make conversation. The adjuster may make some slight comment like, "Oh, well thank goodness you didn't get too hurt," and you may feel the urge to agree with their statement. People tend to shy away from being confrontational, but this is not the place to be shy. You should respond with something like, "I was hurt," not something like, "Yes, thank goodness."

5. Avoid Giving Details of Your Injuries. At this stage of the claim, you should not give many details of the injuries. You can simply say that you will provide reports from your medical providers, which should contain your injuries. Also, it is likely that you do not know for sure the true extent of your injuries, and therefore, it would be hard to specifically say how injured you are. Therefore, if asked about your injuries, you can simply say that you are seeking medical treatment and you can provide the documentation later.

    The adjuster may ask you to list all the medical providers that you have seen since the accident. It's important to list every single one. Not just some of them, but all of them. To stay organized, keep a list of your medical providers that you saw as a result of the accident, that way you can have this available for the statement.

6. Record the Recorded Statement. Before the recorded statement begins, you can state that you want to record the statement as well. During the recorded statement, you can confirm with the adjuster on record that they consent to the recording. That way, you will have the actual recording to use later down the line to recall the details that you gave during your statement. This will be helpful if and when the adjuster tries to use statements you made on the recording against you. Perhaps they were taken out of context or misunderstood, and so you can refute those points at a later time.

7. Remain Calm. This cannot be emphasized on enough. If a person loses their temper during the recorded statement, this can be used throughout the entire claim and litigation. It is better to "keep your cool" and not act and talk irrationally. Speaking with a short fuse can significantly damage your case.

8. Don't Interrupt Each Other. While the adjuster is speaking, remain silent. Wait for them to finish asking their question, and they should wait for you to finish giving your answer. If you speak over each other, this may create many issues. The recording may not be clear, and you may be answering a question that was not asked, potentially harming your case. The best situation is that you listen attentively to what the adjuster is saying and wait for them to finish. If they cut you off, you can politely say, "Please allow me to finish my answer."

9. The Adjuster is Not Your Friend. Insurance adjusters can be really nice people. They can be bubbly over the phone, laugh at all your jokes, and even talk about their own personal lives. They are not your friend! Remember this when they try to get more information from you. It is better to remain professional than to befriend the adjuster who is trying to minimize your case. They are great listeners, and most people love talking about themselves. This is exactly what the adjuster wants you to do. Don't take the bait.

10. Try to Listen More Than You Talk. The adjuster is going to ask how the accident occurred. They will just let you talk and say things to try and minimize your claim. After a little while, they will try and ask clarifying questions. But until then, they will just let you rattle on about every little detail. This is the point where people can start slipping up by offering personal comments, which are irrelevant to the case. They may say things like, "I just broke up with my girlfriend," or, "I was so tired because I was up all night studying for my final." People naturally talk about themselves when they are in a conversation

with someone, and will just talk about all sorts of details. It's important to remember that the insurance adjuster is not your friend. They employ tricks to try and minimize your claim. Down the line, they may refer to these little details that you were talking about in your recorded statement, so they can pin the fault on you.

11. Give A Statement to Your Own Insurance Company. Sometimes, if you are going through your own uninsured/underinsured motorist policy, the insurance company may require you to give a recorded statement if you have a duty to cooperate with them. Sometimes, there is a duty to cooperate in your auto insurance policy. Not cooperating with your own insurance company may harm your uninsured motorist claim. However, just because they are your own insurance company does not mean they are on your side. Clients are often surprised when their own insurance companies give them a hard time when trying to resolve their injury claim.

Don't Settle for the First Offer

Negotiating with the insurance company during the settlement process can be a very difficult task, especially when a person isn't emotionally equipped to handle it. The other side's insurance company will usually try and settle for a lowball offer at first, which can be rather unnerving for a person who feels as though they deserve more for their injuries.

Sometimes, right after taking a recorded statement, an adjuster would like to send a representative out to meet the injured person to talk about settlement. They can try to meet at a public location, like a coffee shop, and talk a little bit about the case. The representative will then offer the injured person a nominal amount on the case, whether it be $500, $1,000, $2000, something very low that "gets rid of them" quickly and inexpensively. This most likely is not the true value of a person's case, but the insurance company's goal is not to make you happy, it's to try to pay you as little as possible.

Receiving a lowball offer can be distressing. The insurance company may offer an amount that is lower than your medical bills, or they may offer nothing at all. A person might feel helpless in settling the case. This is the point that you should make a counter-offer. See Chapter 11, Negotiating a Settlement, for more on this.

Don't Sign a Medical Authorization Without Advice

An insurance company may want you to sign an authorization for medical records. Usually, they are unlimited regarding what information they can seek. This is highly invasive and usually unnecessary. The authorization should be limited to only the injured body parts arising from the accident. Be wary when signing the authorizations, because you don't want to authorize the insurance company to go fishing into your entire medical history.

If the insurance company tries to get you to sign a general medical release, don't sign it immediately. This will essentially allow the insurance company to look at all of your medical history, and go on a "fishing expedition" to find some kind of pre-existing injury or other reasons, which prove that you were not really injured in the accident. There's no real reason to do this at beginning stages of a negotiation, and you don't want to just open up your entire private medical history to the insurance company to get your claim paid. This will eventually allow the insurance company to find any medical document in your history, even if it's not related whatsoever to your injury, and still try to use that against you.

They can try and use embarrassing details (if they exist) about your past to try to pressure you into settling your case, or make you feel like you are not going to get much for your case. Don't be swayed by that if it happens. But to prevent that, limit the authorization to the body parts that were injured in the accident.

If the insurance company is giving you a hard time, then you should either file a lawsuit or hire an attorney to help you with this. The trouble in allowing the insurance company to fish through your entire medical history is that they can unfairly try to minimize your injury, or say that the cause of your injury was something other than the accident.

CHAPTER 6

Statute of Limitations

What is the statute of limitations? The statute of limitations is a deadline to file a lawsuit or perform some action to preserve a party's right to begin a lawsuit. Once that date passes, the lawsuit is likely barred. For different types of cases (such as personal injury, medical malpractice, etc.), there are different statutes of limitations. For different types of defendants (private or public), there are also different statutes of limitations.

Personal Injury

Generally speaking, the statute of limitations for personal injury actions in the State of California is two years from the date of the injury, subject to exceptions. This means that if a person is injured on January 1, they have two years from that date to file a lawsuit. The statute of limitations for personal injury will be applied in the following types of situations:

- Accidents;
- Assault and Battery;
- Intentional or Negligent Infliction of Emotional Distress; and
- Other Negligence

Medical Malpractice

The statute of limitations is complicated in medical malpractice cases. Generally, a person has one year to file a lawsuit from the date the person knows or should have known about the injury, or three years from the date of the injury, whichever is earlier. Code of Civil Procedure Section 340.5.

Essentially, once you learn that you were harmed from the negligence of a medical provider, you need to act within one year of the injury. If you don't find out that you were injured until after three years from the negligence, then your case may be barred.

The facts of a case may alter the statute of limitations to act. If a case is rather complicated, it is probably best to contact a local medical malpractice attorney to assess what the correct statute of limitations is.

Pre-Filing Requirement: Before you sue a medical provider, you must send them a 90-day notice of the patient's intent to file a medical malpractice lawsuit. Here is an example:

"VIA CERTIFIED MAIL

June 1, 20XX

Medical Provider
123 Surgery Lane
Pleasantville, CA 91112

RE: NOTICE PURSUANT TO CCP SECTION 364 RE [Patient's Name]

Dear Medical Provider:

Please allow this letter to serve as notice of my claims against you as the result of the treatment you provided on or about [Date of Negligence]. I contend that you negligently performed [Describe Treatment]. As a result, I did not heal properly and experience pain and suffering.

The purpose of this letter is to advise you that I intend to commence action against you regarding your negligent treatment. This letter is sent to you pursuant to Code of Civil Procedure Section 364.

Sincerely,
[Patient's Name]"

The concept of statute of limitations, when it comes to medical malpractice actions, is a heavily argued issue. Therefore, it is wise to seek legal counsel regarding your statute of limitations deadline.

Injuries to a Minor

There are many peculiar situations in which a personal injury suit must be filed when a minor is involved. Depending on the age and other various factors could cause the date to vary. It is best to consult with a local personal injury attorney to see which deadline applies to the minor, and to act within that deadline to prevent the case from being barred.

Property Damage

In many cases, a person will suffer some kind of property damage. A very common type is in an automobile accident where, aside from the person being injured, their car is damaged as well. In these types of actions, a person has three years from the date of loss to file an action for property damage. This does not extend the two-year statute to file for personal injury. But if the injury claim settles before the property damage claim, then a person will have extra time to file their property damage claim. Usually this claim is filed with a personal injury claim within the two-year statute of limitations.

Government Entities

One has to make special considerations if the potential defendant in a lawsuit is a government entity or employee. First, there is a different statute of limitations. Instead of two years from the date of the injury, the deadline runs at six months for personal injury claims. Also, the filing procedure is not as simple.

This section applies to suing the California government. Suing the federal government or other governments have different sets of rules. It can be extremely complicated to sue the government and it is not recommended to sue the government without the assistance of an attorney.

CHAPTER 7

Gathering Your Evidence

Gathering evidence is important for two reasons. First, it allows you to prepare your settlement demand package, and second, it prepares you for a lawsuit if your claim goes in that direction. Here, we will go through many types of evidence that you can use to raise your personal injury claim's value.

Medical Records

When trying to resolve your personal injury matter, you're going to want copies of all your medical records. These records will entail your injury diagnosis, your treatment, and the future course of your injury and treatment. This is extremely important for your personal injury claim because your words alone, without medical documentation or a provider backing it up, may have little weight.

If you don't have your medical records, request your provider to give them to you. Read through them to make sure they do not contain any errors. If they contain errors, you can contact the medical provider and request that they correct the errors in the records or medical report. If you are going to need future treatment, and your medical records do not indicate that, you should ask your provider to include what future medical treatment they recommend and how much it is going to cost in their report about you.

Gathering your medical records can involve a lot of work, but this is what it takes to raise your claim's value. If you're juggling with many medical providers, and your injuries are substantial, keep a detailed list of your medical providers. If it is too much for you to handle, or you simply need the extra help, then you may want to consider hiring an attorney to help organize and gather your medical data and negotiate your claim with the other side. You may overlook some important information, which could vastly change your case's value.

Medical Bills

When requesting your medical records, request the bills as well. The bills will show what the outstanding balance is on your claim. These are a part of the damages in your personal injury claim. Before making the demand, you should make sure that the bills are up to date to further ensure accuracy when presenting your claim.

After you receive the bills, make a spreadsheet and add up your bills. This way, you know what the total medical bills are in your case and this can give you an indication on how much to ask for and settle for. Here is an example:

Provider	Billed Amount
Dr. Simon – Orthopedist	$5,000
Dr. Rubin – Chiropractor	$2,500
Pharmacy	$112.50
TOTAL	$7,612.50

Sample Letter Requesting Medical Records and Bills

For your convenience, see the following template of a letter requesting medical bills and records:

"VIA FIRST CLASS MAIL

June 1, 20XX

Dr. Simon
Simon Orthopedics

123 Treatment Lane
Medicalville, CA 91112

Name:	Iman Pain
Date of Birth:	June 1, 1965
Social Security Number:	123-45-6789
Dates of Treatment:	March 1, 20XX–May 21, 20XX

REQUEST FOR MEDICAL RECORDS AND BILLS

To Whom It May Concern:

Please allow this letter to serve as a formal request for my medical records and bills. The requested medical records and bills pertain to the dates of treatment listed above. This should include all bills, records, notes, reports, evaluations, pictures, X-rays, MRIs, and any other documentation associated with my treatment.

Please let me know what the fee is for a copy of my records. Please prepare my records so that I may obtain them within 30 days. When they are gathered, please mail them to me at [*Insert address here*].

I look forward to hearing from you at your earliest convenience. Thank you for your anticipated cooperation. If you have any questions, please call me at [*Insert phone number here*].

Sincerely,
Iman Pain

Insurance Payments – Explanation of Benefits (EOBs)

If you have insurance, either private or public (like Medicare), it's important to include how much they paid for your treatments. They may assert a lien, so it's important to make sure of that and the lien amount before settling the case. You don't want to be stuck with an insurance company or other lien creditor chasing you down after settling your claim. You should include the payment information from the insurance companies, as this will be evidence and part of how much compensation the other side should be responsible for.

The explanations of benefits (EOBs) are documents that entail how much your health insurance company paid out on a certain claim for specific dates of service. This number is helpful in aggregating what your total damages are regarding the medical bills.

These documents should be gathered as they can be used to show how much your insurance company may be paid back. If your insurance company paid out a certain amount on a claim, they may want reimbursement on that claim. You may want to call your health insurance and ask them whether your insurance is requesting reimbursement on the claim.

If they state that they are not going to request reimbursement, you should document this in writing. Here is a sample letter:

"VIA FIRST CLASS MAIL

June 1, 20XX

Adjuster
Health Insurance Company
555 Claims Lane
Fair Billing, CA 90055

Name:	Iman Pain
Date of Birth:	June 1, 1965
Social Security Number:	123-45-6789
Dates of Treatment:	March 1, 20XX – May 21, 20XX
Claim Number:	98765-4321A

Dear Adjuster:

This is to confirm our conversation over the telephone today where you indicated to me that [the Name of Insurance Company] is not requesting reimbursement on the above-referenced claim. Please contact me right away if this is inaccurate information.

Sincerely,
Iman Pain"

Different insurance entities may have specific authorizations and request forms for their medical records. If you belong to an insurance company that requires a specific authorization, you can obtain such authorization from the company, and fill it out according to their specific format.

Photographs of the Accident

You should gather photographs of the accident as part of your evidence. Hopefully you read this book in time, or were well prepared beforehand and knew to take many pictures shortly after the accident occurred. This evidence should include photographs of the following:

- How the accident occurred: skid marks, broken parts and glass;
- The actual accident: whether it be a car accident, slip and fall, dog bite, or whatever accident you were involved with;
- The participants and witnesses: including police officers;
- Weather conditions (more applicable in outdoor cases, like car accidents); and
- Any injuries and property damage (include close-up and distance shots).

If you were involved in a car accident, you may have pictures of both cars, any tire skid marks, any property damage, injuries, and photographs showing how the accident occurred. If you take more pictures, then the chances of having clear, unmistakably good pictures are higher, which are going to be helpful in your claim.

If you were involved in a slip and fall and were able to take pictures, you should take pictures of what you slipped on and how you slipped. You can also take pictures of reference points from different angles to show the area where you slipped.

These examples are simply to get your imagination going as to how many pictures and what kinds of pictures you should be gathering.

Low Property Damage

Oftentimes, the insurance company will base their claim on the property damage involved in an accident. In a car accident case, the insurance company may base their claim on the impact of the car. So, for lower property damage cases, the insurance company will likely give a harder time about paying an adequate amount for the injury. As an aside, I've seen many cases where there is lower property damage, but the person did suffer significant bodily injuries. This may occur when a person is driving a rather safe car, and the impact on that car may not cause as much property damage as it would in a car that may have a weaker frame. Even though the impact may cause low property damage, the accident may cause significant injuries to the person. There are cases where a person suffers relatively low property damage, but recovered a lot of money for their injuries.

Photographs of Injuries

Photographs of the injury are important in a personal injury case. Photographs should be taken at the time of the injury, and progression photographs should be taken until the injury heals. Take enough to show the status and progression of the injury.

If the injuries to a person are gruesome, this will likely add value to the case. If you have suffered an injury, which is visible to the eye, even if it is a bruise, you should take pictures of those injuries.

Keep in mind that these photographs will likely end up in the hands of the other side. When taking pictures of injuries, you can follow some of these helpful tips:

- **Take the picture in a clean area**: If you are taking a picture in a dirty room, then the focus may move away from your injury and onto the clutter.
- **Casts, braces, and wheelchairs**: If you require an accessory, you should take pictures with those accessories.
- **Don't smile**: This makes your injury appear not as serious if you smile.

- **Close-up and distant**: Zoom in and out of the injuries. You should be able to give the other side a lot of perspective as to how serious the injuries are.
- **Be formal**: Don't wear makeup or jewelry, and dress conservatively.
- **Entire body**: Even if the injury does not pertain to the entire body, it is good to take such pictures because it gives perspective.

If your medical providers have copies of pictures, X-rays, MRIs, or any other depiction of the injuries, you should request copies of those from the medical providers. You can use the letter provided earlier in the chapter to obtain such records.

Whiplash cases: In cases where you are suffering an injury that cannot be seen, then photographs regarding the injuries may not be as helpful. Regarding other injuries, like broken bones, those can be seen using proper technology. If you have suffered a soft tissue injury, you should be very specific in your demand as to how the injury affected your life.

Police Report

We have an entire chapter devoted to the police report, but we will briefly touch upon the subject here, as it can be a rather vital piece of evidence, both before litigation and after the litigation has begun. What the officer can do is come out to the scene of the incident and gather witness statements, and then deduce how the accident happened.

Police reports serve several functions. One is that they can show how the accident occurred, and then help to establish liability. The other is that they can help justify the injuries suffered by stating how great of an impact the accident was, whether the people were injured because of the accident, and the officer's thoughts about the injuries. Third, they may contain witness information that you were not able to gather. The police report, especially if it is favorable to your case, should be obtained.

There are several ways to obtain the police report. You can call the police or sheriff's department, which took down the information from the incident, and ask them what their procedure is. You can follow the procedural steps to obtain the report. Oftentimes, different departments have different procedures for obtaining information. For more information on the police report, including altering certain pieces of information, see the chapter "Police Reports."

Proof of Lost Wages

If you have suffered lost wages due to your injury, you should gather this evidence as well. This can be in the form of paystubs, a letter from the employer, or if you're self-employed, profit and loss statements from a third party, or something that proves you had actually suffered lost wages. You'll want to gather this evidence and include it in your settlement demand package.

Proof of Loss of Earning Capacity

Loss of earning capacity, or loss of future wages, is a slightly complicated matter. This evidence can come in several forms, and we touch upon it in the chapter "Compensation for Your Injury Claim." Loss of earning capacity in a personal injury case requires proof with reasonable certainty that a person is not going to be able to work. Therefore, you should hire experts, both medical and vocational, to show that despite your talents and skills, which you had before the injury, you will not be able to work such jobs that would require those talents and skills until you heal, if you heal at all.

If you are experiencing a loss of earning capacity, you may want to seek legal counsel. These are somewhat more complicated than your average whiplash personal injury cases, and the insurance company will likely be less than willing to pay the adequate compensation on a loss of earning capacity claim without litigation. Therefore, you may want to consider hiring an attorney.

Nonetheless, you should be gathering this evidence, and it can be in the following forms (this is not an exhaustive list):

- Paystubs;
- Medical reports showing how long you will be out of work;

- Expert reports or testimonies indicating what your skills and talents were, and how much you would be getting paid for those jobs, had you been able to work.

Witness Statements

Witness statements may be helpful in showing how your accident occurred and/or the extent of your injuries. They are very important in helping prove your case since they present a different point of view than the injured person.

You are better off gathering witness statements sooner rather than later, while the witnesses' memories of the accident are still fresh. The longer a person waits after the accident to take a witness statement, the more likely it is that the witness is not going to remember all the details of what happened in the accident. It's almost useless to you if you call a witness and they simply don't remember what happened in the accident.

If you call the witness and they act unfavorably towards you, then you probably should not take down their statement and hand it over to the other side. Additionally, you should not call that witness to any court hearing or trial.

In the witness statement, you'll want to include a statement of their perspective as to how the accident occurred. You can include what they were doing before, during, and after the accident regarding witnessing it.

Here are some additional tips when dealing with a witness who is a stranger:

- **Be friendly**: Don't frighten the witness by being overly aggressive. Witnesses are often afraid to come forward. If the witness seems afraid, stay calm and try to gain some rapport with them. Witnesses are incredibly helpful.
- **Get contact information:** Get all their information—name, address, phone number(s), email, and other information they hand over.

- **Ask what they saw**: Ask what they saw before, during, and after the accident.
- **If favorable, ask whether they will sign a statement**: This is pretty simple, and I've included a few samples below.

Witness statements may be less helpful in certain situations, like if the person is your relative, if they have a financial interest in the case, or if the person knew you before the accident. This is not to say that their statements will not be helpful at all, but they will have less impact than a statement from a witness' who does not know you personally in any way.

Sample Witness Statement Who Saw An Auto Accident:

"I, John Smith, an individual who resides in the State of California, hereby state the following:

1. I was driving down the 405 freeway at 5:30 p.m. on July 5, 20XX after work.
2. The weather was sunny with no clouds.
3. I was driving next to the cement barrier, in the lane going southbound near the Wilshire Boulevard exit.
4. There was heavy traffic, and the cars in all lanes had come to a complete stop in front of me, so I started to slow down.
5. I saw a green Ford (License Plate No. 1ABC123) driven by Mr. Iman Pain, which was at a complete stop in the lane next to mine.
6. As I slowed down, I saw a red Lexus (License Plate No. 2XYZ456), driven by Yura T. Fault, rear end Mr. Pain's car. Mr. Fault was driving at approximately 30 miles per hour when he hit Mr. Pain's car. I believe Mr. Fault caused the accident, since Mr. Pain was at a complete stop like the cars in front of him.
7. I got out of my car to see if everyone was all right. Mr. Pain complained of back and neck pain, and that he was rather sore. Mr. Fault kept saying, "I'm so sorry, I'm so sorry."

8. I gave both Mr. Fault and Mr. Pain my contact information. My address is 123 Witness Lane, Los Angeles, CA 90045. My phone number is 213-111-1122.

Signed: John Smith
Dated: July 31, 20XX"

If you can't get a hold of the witness on the telephone, you can send them a physical letter or email requesting a witness statement. Here is a sample letter requesting such statement:

"VIA US MAIL

July 10, 20XX

John Smith
123 Witness Lane
Los Angeles, CA 90045
213-111-1122

Re: Car Accident on July 5, 20XX

Dear Mr. Smith:

I am writing to you regarding the above-referenced matter. I noticed that you were a witness to this incident and would like to request a statement from you. Please give me a call or simply fill out the bottom of this page and return it to me at [Insert Your Address Here].

Sincerely,
Iman Pain

Name of Witness:
Witness Address:
Witness Phone Number:
Date of Incident:
Location of Incident:

Please describe how the event occurred:

I declare that the statement above is true and correct to the best of my knowledge.

Signature: Dated: "

Expert Reports

An expert report is an extremely useful tool in a personal injury matter. The expert report, although it is likely hearsay evidence by itself, will show the other side what an expert says concerning the personal injury matter. Although helpful, expert reports are often expensive. Therefore, it is sometimes useful to hire an attorney who has dealt or regularly deals with experts.

To obtain an expert report, contact your expert to set up an evaluation. There are many experts from whom you can obtain reports. Each type of expert and their area of expertise is beyond the scope of this book, however, I will briefly describe many of the very common ones.

Medical expert: This type of expert should detail your injuries, if the accident caused the injury, your treatment, and what your future treatment will entail and what it will cost.

Economist: This type of expert is used for several functions. If you are going to need a lot of care in the future, then they can calculate the costs of those future cares. Additionally, if you have past or future lost wages, they can calculate what those lost wages are going to be.

Accident Reconstructionist: This type of expert can put together how an accident occurred. This type of expert can be helpful if you have an unsatisfactory police report that you want to argue against.

Life Care Planner: This type of expert can put together an analysis of all the care (medical and supplies) that you may need in the future. They can collect reports from other experts to put together an analysis of what your future is going to look like due to the injury.

There are many types of experts who serve many functions. If your damages are severe enough, you may want to consider hiring an attorney to help you with your case.

CHAPTER 8

Compensation for an Injury Claim

This chapter was placed here to prepare you for what to look for prior to writing your demand letter to the other side or their insurance company. This is to prepare you for the types of damages that may be available to your claim. There are several types of compensation that a person can recover from their personal injury claim including but not limited to pain and suffering, medical bills, and lost wages.

Pain and Suffering (Past and Future)

In many personal injury cases, people will refer to what's called "pain and suffering." But what does that really mean? People often have a preconceived notion as to what pain and suffering means, but there's actually a guideline in which pain and suffering is realized, and that is how attorneys can increase a case's value. It's important to realize that "pain and suffering" is a somewhat abstract term, meaning that it's not exactly a black-and-white term.

Usually, people have to use a case's facts and circumstances in order to justify a more valuable or less valuable "pain and suffering." "Pain and suffering" can essentially establish the pain, mental anguish and emotional distress that a person endures after being injured in an accident.

An entire book can be devoted to defining "pain and suffering" since it encompasses so many different scenarios and ways to value it. Generally, "pain and suffering" can be broken down into several categories.

1. Actual pain

If a person feels actual pain, this is going to positively affect their "pain and suffering" value. If a person feels pain after an accident, it's important to make a note of it, especially in their demand letter. If a person, after treatment, still feels a lot of pain, then it is important to highlight that in their settlement demand down the line.

For example, let's say a person slips and falls in a restaurant due to someone's negligence and breaks their knee. After extensive evaluation, the victim's surgeon says that they are going to experience pain for the rest of their life. The pain is going to be moderate. The moderate pain that a person experiences every single day has a value to it. But what is that value? It is usually the trial attorney's job of arguing that value to the jury. In larger cases, like where a person is going to have significant pain for the rest of their life, it is recommend that the victim hire an attorney since the insurance company is very unlikely to give a fair settlement to someone without representation.

One strategy that a person can do is ask, "How much should this person be paid for every day of pain? $10? $20?" Additionally, the rest of their life needs to be calculated, for which we have tables to work with, and they can be found in the Judicial Council of California Civil Jury Instructions (CACI). Now if the victim is 35 and is going to live until 75, that is 40 years of pain that the victim may have to endure. The value of that pain adds up significantly. In these types of complicated cases, it is a good idea to get the assistance of a competent attorney with extensive experience in this field.

In soft tissue cases (such as whiplash, sore back and neck), it is unlikely that a person will be feeling pain for the rest of their life. Also, if a person argues that they are going to be in pain when they really are not, this may negatively impact their credibility, which also affects the case's value (especially if they say something similar in their recorded statement or in court).

In soft tissue cases, it is best not to exaggerate the pain levels, but to be very upfront about any pain you are experiencing. A good indication of a person's pain is what is reported in the medical reports. When you go to your medical provider, tell the provider the pain that you are experiencing, and be specific. When it comes to a person's pain, it is best not to underplay or try to appear tough in a personal injury matter. At the same time, it is best not to exaggerate. Just be forthcoming and honest.

Take photographs. If you have visible pain symptoms, like bruises or gashes, you should take pictures, many of them. This can also play a role in adding value to your case. The insurance companies know that a judge or jury is going to react to photographs. So, the more graphic and severe an injury looks, the more value that pain likely has. Since insurance companies know this, they may be willing to pay you more if you have decent photographs to attach to your settlement demand package, or to bring with you to court.

2. Emotional distress

After an accident, a victim may experience sadness, depression, anxiety, panic, or other emotional distress that affects their life negatively. These are generally the psychological impacts that an injury has on you. These kinds of mental anguish can positively affect the value of "pain and suffering" as well.

If you believe that you suffer from severe emotional distress, seek the help of a professional. Not only should this help you personally, but it should also help your personal injury matter. If you see a therapist, psychologist, psychiatrist or any other mental health professional, it's important to make note that in the demand letter, and request reimbursement for the sessions. If a person seeks mental health help, it may add more value to a case (as long as it was reasonably necessary) than a person who claims they suffered emotional distress, but did not seek psychological help.

An example of a person experiencing emotional distress is a person bit by a dog in the face. If they suffer a significant scar on their face, they have to go outside and face people in the world every day and feel the embarrassment from that scar. Everywhere they go, people may do a double take when they see the person, which makes them embarrassed and extremely insecure. Before the accident, they may have been a very attractive person, but now they suffer humiliation when nearly every person they come across may stare or glance at their scar. They may lose a sense of their former identity due to the dog bite. A person like this may suffer severe emotional distress, and that may add significant value to the case.

If a person suffered severe emotional distress, they could potentially sue for "intentional infliction of emotional distress" (IIED), which is entirely separate and can be an addition to suing for "negligence." Essentially, intentional infliction of emotional distress means that the other side acted with extreme or outrageous behavior, and intentionally or recklessly caused severe emotional distress to the victim. One example of this is where a nurse calls a patient's family, telling them that the patient had passed, knowing that the patient is still alive, for the purpose of harassing the family. IIED arises in peculiar situations and is usually a tough sell to a judge or jury. Suing for IIED after a car accident due to someone's negligence is usually an uphill battle and not recommended. If you believe your case may truly fall under IIED, you should consult with a competent attorney.

Generally speaking, the more emotionally distressed a person is, the more value the emotional distress can add to their case. Obviously, there are exceptions, such as if a person has a pre-existing mental condition, which causes them to experience more severe emotional distress. This is not to say that a person with a pre-existing condition can't recover, but recovering without a pre-existing mental condition is simpler.

If you were in a car accident, you may be afraid of driving. If you are, make this trauma a part of your demand. If you were bit by a dog and are now terrified of dogs or walking by yourself or some other fear that the dog bite caused you, mention that.

3. Medical bills

An important factor that drives the argument of pain and suffering is the amount of medical bills. For example, if a person underwent surgery, their medical bills could be worth $10,000 or more. If a person made a few visits to the chiropractor or physical therapist, their medical bills may be under $10,000. A person who has to undergo surgery is more likely going to have more "pain and suffering" than someone who goes for physical therapy.

However, the "pain and suffering" will likely be balanced against the reasonable value of the treatment and not what the provider bills for. If the physical therapist charges $1,000 per visit, where the reasonable value may be $100, the "pain and suffering" would more likely be associated with the $100 and not the $1,000. On the flipside, if a person goes to a surgeon and is charged $1,000, they will likely have more "pain and suffering" compared to the person who goes to the physical therapist who charged the same price. This is because the value of the surgeon appointment is likely much more than the value of the physical therapist appointment.

You can't just show the other side's insurance company, the judge or jury a copy of your bills and say, "This is how much pain and suffering I had!" The medical bills are a factor of the "pain and suffering" to show how much treatment and healing you had to go through in order to get to where you are.

4. Loss of Consortium – Loss of Love and Sex

Loss of consortium comes into play in more severe cases. There are two types of loss of consortium: one is the loss of love, companion, society, and comfort of a loved one, and the other is the loss of enjoyment of sexual relations or the ability to have children. Usually, a spouse will claim loss of consortium if their other spouse cannot participate in their marriage relationship like they used to prior to the injury due to the injury.

This is essentially what the non-injured spouse endures due to their spouse's injury. Loss of consortium claims can have significant value, as the loss of love and sex can have an extremely emotional impact on a spouse's life. If you believe you are experiencing a loss of consortium claim due to yours or your spouse's injuries, it is probably best to hire a personal injury attorney as these can be more complicated cases. They may have higher value, and insurance companies will likely make you jump through major legal hoops to get a fair recovery.

5. Nature and Extent of the Injuries

Personal injury cases are usually divided into two categories: soft-tissue injuries and hard injuries. These two types of injuries vary greatly in how they are valued, but also in how they are litigated. Soft-tissue injuries usually involve some type of soreness that a person is experiencing. Hard-tissue injuries usually involve injuries that are evidenced in medical examinations, like broken bones or torn tissues.

Whiplash cases, cases that involve a person's pain and discomfort, are soft tissue cases for the most part. They involve going to a few doctor and other medical provider visits until they are completely healed. The medical provider's reports will usually show evidence based on the patient's statements that they are feeling pain, but now are able to actually show the physical cause of the pain. These cases usually have a lower settlement value than a hard-injury case.

A person who suffers from a whiplash will likely have a different "pain and suffering" than someone who suffers from broken limbs. Certainly, there are very wide separations between the extent of people's injuries. Generally, the more injured a person is, the more value the "pain and suffering" aspect of the case will be.

6. Duration of the Treatment and Recovery

The duration that a person is in treatment and the time it takes to recover, are factors in determining the value of "pain and suffering." People have varying degrees regarding how long their treatment is going to last. For example, a person who has suffered a soft-tissue injury may go to physical therapy for a few months. A person who suffers broken limbs may have a longer treatment and recovery period. Some people who unfortunately suffer paralysis of some sort, or some kind of nerve damage, will sometimes never recover, which would add significant value to their case. The general rule here is that the longer the treatment is going to be, and the longer the road to recovery, the more valuable a case will be in terms of "pain and suffering."

The big question is: how do we value this aspect of "pain and suffering"? If a person suffers from paralysis of their arms, what is the value to that person? In more serious cases like these, it is better to hire an attorney to help litigate that type of "pain and suffering," since it is going to be significant, and insurance companies are rarely going to play fair and pay the reasonable value of such an injury without a fight.

If a person is injured for a few months, or even weeks, their "pain and suffering" damages are going to be relatively low. Even if an insurance company offers a somewhat lower offer than what a person would expect for their "pain and suffering," they may not want to go through the trouble of a lawsuit to get a few more dollars, so they may take the deal. In smaller cases, lawyers and victims of injuries are more hesitant to go to court over a relatively low amount of "pain and suffering," and the insurance companies are well aware of this. However, you should always let them know that you are willing to go to court. In smaller cases, you can go to small claims court, which is a relatively simple procedure and a mere fraction of the work involved in superior court litigation. The willingness to go to litigation, despite quick recovery of an injury, can add value to your personal injury case.

7. Photographs of Property Damage

Property damage can affect the value of a person's pain and suffering. You may be wondering why damage to the vehicle is relevant to a person's "pain and suffering."

Property damage plays a role in assessing whether the accident could have caused the injury. Property damage can also play a role in the severity of an impact, and how a judge or jury may react to the photographs. If a vehicle is more damaged, then a judge or jury will react differently compared to if a vehicle is less damaged. Insurance companies know this, and they use this factor in their assessment to value a case of "pain and suffering."

However, there are situations where there is little property damage and a person is very injured. These are more difficult cases because an adjuster will judge a person's injuries based on the property damage. If a car looks like it has barely been hit, the victim could still suffer serious injuries and be in pain for a long time. If your case falls into this low property damage category, consulting with an attorney is probably a good idea if and when the insurance company starts giving you a hard time about your injuries. There have been circumstances when there was significantly low property damage, but a victim was able to recover a large amount of "pain and suffering" compensation.

Nonetheless, you should have photographs of the property damage. Therefore, when the time comes, your evidence will be ready.

8. Documenting Your Pain and Suffering

Take notes, as much as you can, about your pain and suffering. You should take notes so that you can recall what you were feeling, and the pain and suffering you were going through, when the time comes. Here are some suggestions:

- Document your pain: Take pictures of visible symptoms. What are you feeling? On a scale of 1–10, how bad is your pain? What is the date, time, and location of where you were feeling the pain? What were you doing at the time? Has this prevented you from doing what you love?
- Document your emotions: What emotional distress are you feeling? Are you sad, angry, anxious, or embarrassed? What happened to you that caused these emotions?
- Document your loss of consortium: Is your spouse unavailable physically, mentally or emotionally because of the injury? Are you unavailable? Has your intimate life or companionship suffered because of the injury? How so?

Past and Future Lost Wages

A person is entitled to lost wages if the injury caused the person to miss work and lose wages. If a person is in a car accident, and has to take three weeks off of work, then they are entitled to three weeks worth of wages. There are several ways of proving the loss of wages. Usually, the insurance company that's being negotiated with will want proof of the lost wages. This is in the form of either a letter from the employer, copies of prior paystubs showing how much a person is being paid, and the like. When a person is ready to settle their personal injury matter, they can include the proof of the lost wages in their settlement demand package.

If a person is self-employed, it's more difficult to prove lost wages. This is because their wages are generally more speculative than a person who is getting a steady paycheck. This is not to say that a self-employed person cannot recover lost wages, but rather it is a more difficult hurdle, and insurance companies are more reluctant to pay lost wages to someone who is self-employed. The way that a person who is self-employed would prove the lost wages is by showing evidence of loss and the work that they could have performed had it not been for the accident.

Loss of Earning Capacity

A person can also claim loss of earning capacity, or future lost wages. To recover this, the injured has to prove the amount of money they are reasonably certain to have earned if they were not injured. This is somewhat difficult to prove, and it is not necessary to have a work history to prove this.

An example of this would be if a person is in an accident and has lost use of their leg. Their ability to work on a job, which would require using their leg, would now be impaired.

To show loss of earning capacity, you may look at the following factors:

- Hiring an expert to determine whether a person would, in fact, not be able to work on tasks involving their injury;
- Assessing a person's skills and experience; and
- Calculating the wages that a person would have recovered on certain jobs had they not been injured.

For a person to recover future lost wages, they need to prove those wages with some degree of certainty. To accomplish this, a personal injury victim will need to use two sources of information: medical and employment. First, from the medical side, they are going to need to know approximately for how long they are going to be out of work, and that the accident caused them the inability to work. Second, from the employment side, they are going to need to know how much they would have made had they been working. Using those two bits of information, the victim can come up with a rough estimate as to how much future lost wages they should be claiming.

Loss of earning capacity is a complicated calculation, it will likely require the help of experts, and it is probably best to hire an attorney if you believe your injury is going to prevent you from being able to work effectively in the future.

Past and Future Medical Costs

Past Medical Costs

A person who is injured at the fault of another is entitled to the reasonable value of the medical treatment that was reasonable and necessary due to the accident. Why is the term "reasonable" used so much? If a person is injured, they should not rack up an exorbitant amount of bills for medical treatment, which they don't need, and expect to be compensated. Instead, they should be reasonable about getting treatment, and get it for a reasonable cost.

How does a person determine the "reasonable value" of services? The answer is somewhat complicated. It depends on who the provider is and what they are charging for their services. The insurance company can respond after a settlement offer, see the amount of medical bills charged, and give a lower offer claiming that the amount on the bills is not the reasonable value.

For settlement purposes, if the insurance company responds to an offer claiming that the medical bills submitted are not of reasonable value, you should be able to respond with the correct facts indicating that the bills submitted are the reasonable value. Be prepared with your response. You can point to factors such as the following:

- The amount billed;
- The amount that the patient is responsible for;

- The amount paid; and
- The amount that other providers in the geographic area would charge for the same services.

To help prove the reasonable value of services, you may need to get a doctor or medical billing expert to testify for you. If the claim is significant enough, meaning that the costs of the treatment are very high, then it may be better to seek an attorney's help.

Before litigation, a person doesn't have to prove to the court or jury by expert testimony of what the actual reasonable value is, since they are just submitting the bills to the other side's insurance. So, what a person really needs to do before a litigation, if they want to settle their claim, is to settle for an amount that resolves all medical bills, pain and suffering, and any other damages they are claiming (such as lost wages).

For example: Rubin settles his personal injury claim for $5,000. Dr. Simon has a lien for $4,000. Rubin offers Dr. Simon to resolve the lien for the amount of $2,500. Dr. Simon accepts. Rubin is able to settle his claim, pay Dr. Simon $2,500 and take $2,500 for himself.

Abuse in the Medical Field: Many attorneys will send their clients to doctor upon doctor, upon other providers, to get the medical bills extraordinarily high, and when the insurance company declines to pay, the attorneys dump their clients and leave them with thousands (if not more) in medical bills, which they may be liable for. Unfortunately, this kind of medical treatment abuse is prevalent in the personal injury field. Therefore, the law is devised in a way that a person's entitlement to compensation for their medical bills is the reasonable value of reasonable services.

Future Medical Costs

Future medical costs are obtainable in a personal injury matter. However, they must be proven with some degree of certainty. Most times, if not all the time, this is done through either expert reports or testimonies.

For example, if a person is going to need surgery, but is not eligible to get the surgery right away, we can send them to the surgeon for a consultation and request that they send us a report, which includes the future surgery's cost. That documentation can be sent to the other side's insurance company so that they can assess how much the claim is worth, and put that in their calculation of how much they will offer as compensation.

Future medical costs can become very complicated. If a person has a severe injury, such as paralysis, they will likely require a lot of future care. They may require physical and mental therapies, medications, in-home care, and other future medical care. Dealing with many experts can become complicated, and there are several strategies to deal with many of them. The experts can all send their reports to a life-care planner and an economist to add everything up, then you can present all the reports to the insurance company. However, this becomes very complicated, and if your injury is severe enough that you are going to need all of those experts, it is better to talk to a competent attorney. It is likely in this type of case that you are going to have to file a lawsuit to get your fair compensation.

Cap on Damages in Medical Malpractice Cases

In the State of California, medical malpractice "pain and suffering" has a cap of $250,000. The Medical Injury Compensation Reform Act (MICRA), was a law that put this cap of medical malpractice "pain and suffering" at $250,000.

If there are "economic damages," such as lost wages or future care, then you may be able to recover for those damages, and get around the $250,000 cap. If a person is no longer able to work, due to the negligence of a medical provider, you can sue for lost wages and request that amount be added to the total award.

Punitive Damages

In some cases, a victim of personal injury can obtain "punitive damages," which generally means they are damages to punish the other side's wrongdoings. To obtain punitive damages, a person or entity may need to be liable for some kind of conduct which includes malice, oppression, or fraud. This is a tough burden, and you are not likely going to get punitive damages in your ordinary accident case where a person makes a mistake and causes the accident. Punitive damages typically involve some kind of assault, battery, or willful misconduct.

Property Damage

A person can recover the reasonable value of the damage to their property. If a person is in a car accident, they should be able to recover the reasonable value to put their car back in the position that it was in before the accident. What typically happens in personal injury matters is the car will be sent to a body shop, and one of the insurance companies will pay for the car to be fixed.

CHAPTER 9

Liens

What is a Lien?

A lien simply means that you are giving someone a right to be paid from the financial recovery. There are many types of liens on a personal injury case. The most common liens are medical provider liens. For instance, if the injured person signs a lien contract with a medical provider granting them a lien against the injured person's case, it means that once there is a financial recovery, the medical provider must be paid from the case according to the lien amount. The most common types of liens and many issues involving liens will be discussed here.

Private Medical Provider Lien

Often, when a person gets into an accident of some sort, they need medical attention. However, not everyone can afford medical treatment. If a person is injured and needs treatment, there are several ways to financially cover that treatment. Many times, a medical provider will agree to treat a personal injury victim on a "lien."

When it's time to financially resolve the injured person's case, the medical provider can be contacted to discuss their lien amount. What has happened many times is that the injured or their attorney will ask the medical provider to reduce their lien amount, based on the settlement offer from the at-fault insurance company, so that they can settle the case. This scenario can play out in many different ways. The medical provider can accept the reduction, or they can reject it. If they reject the reduction, it's still possible to settle, but an attorney should be consulted so that the injured person can avoid litigation with the medical provider.

For example: Rubin gets into a car accident. Rubin sees Dr. Simon and signs a lien contract granting Dr. Simon a lien against Rubin's personal injury matter. Dr. Simon charges Rubin $10,000 for treatment. Rubin gets a settlement offer for $15,000. Rubin calls Dr. Simon and requests Dr. Simon to reduce his lien to $7,500. That way, Rubin can keep $7,500. Dr. Simon can either accept or reject the reduction.

What happens very often in personal injury matters is that if the injured retained an attorney, then the attorney, medical provider, and injured will all split the settlement offer into thirds.

Example: Rubin gets into a car accident. Rubin hires an attorney. Rubin gets sent to Dr. Simon for treatment. Rubin signs a contract with Dr. Simon granting Dr. Simon a lien against Rubin's settlement. Dr. Simon sign it and charges Rubin $10,000 for treatment. The attorney contacts the insurance company and gets a settlement offer of $15,000. The attorney can contact Dr. Simon and request that Dr. Simon reduce his lien to $5,000, so that the attorney can take $5,000, and the client can take $5,000. Once everyone accepts, the case can be settled.

When Does a Lien Get Placed on Your Case?

Usually, an injured person agrees to grant some entity (like a medical provider) a lien on their case by signing a lien contract. However, sometimes liens get placed on personal injury cases even without the injured person's consent. When it comes to hospitals, child support, and other "statutory liens," a lien may be placed on an injured person's case, and if they collect money without paying off the lien, legal trouble can ensue.

If a lawyer forgets to pay off a lien, a medical provider can sue both the lawyer and the client for payment.

Medicare or Medicaid (Medi-Cal) Lien

If a person is being treated under Medicare or California's Medi-Cal, then those entities will have a right to reimbursement for expenses that they paid out for the victim's treatment. They have very specific procedures regarding lien reimbursement. They may accept a reduction of their lien after following their specific format. Although they may take some time to resolve a person's lien, it can save a lot of money down the line.

Child Support Lien

If a personal injury case owes child support, that can affect their personal injury claim. The insurance company may get notice of the child support lien, and disbursing settlement sums may become difficult. To negotiate the child support lien, the child support services should be contacted and negotiated with.

Workers' Compensation Lien

Workers' compensation liens are tricky matters. If a person is injured on the job and a third-party component is involved, then both workers' compensation and the third party's insurance (or their own insurance) may be financially involved.

For example: Rubin is working as a gas station attendant. While at work, Simon negligently hits Rubin with his car. Rubin opens a workers' compensation claim with his employer's workers' compensation insurance, and a personal injury claim with Simon's insurance company.

Many times, the workers' compensation insurance company will give benefits pertaining to the victim's lost wages and medical treatment. The victim may not collect the entirety of those amounts from the third party's insurance company since that would be considered double dipping, and the workers' compensation insurance company may require reimbursement.

To know the ins and outs of what to do in this situation, you should get a copy of the workers' compensation insurance policy to know what their rights are in terms of reimbursement, and what you can recover from the other side's insurance company. Since this is a rather tricky situation, it may be best to consult with an attorney.

Resolving Liens on Your Personal Injury Case

There is a strategy to resolving personal injury liens on your case. This is incredibly helpful so that you are not out of pocket for your medical bills, and so the medical providers and other entities don't come after you after settling your personal injury case. When you start the settlement procedures, you should keep your liens in mind.

Step One: Know What Liens Are On Your Case.

You should have a file of all the liens that are on your case. Perhaps you saw an orthopedic surgeon, a chiropractor, and a physical therapist, who all have liens on your case. You should make sure that you have copies of the lien agreements as well.

Before submitting your settlement demand, you should get the latest copies of outstanding bills with each lienholder. That way, you know how much you owe and how much to negotiate on each bill.

Step Two: Contact Each Lien Claimant and Let Them Know You Are Settling the Case Before You Actually Settle

If you have an offer with the insurance company, you can let the lien claimant know that you are close to settling the case, but will need a reduction on the lien to completely resolve the matter. The reason why this is complex is because not every lien claimant is going to accept a reduction, and if this stalls your settlement process, you may need to contact an attorney to smooth things over.

You can either make a phone call, or write a letter to the lien claimant requesting a reduction. Here is an example of a lien reduction request. It is very similar to negotiating a settlement with the insurance company or opposing party in an accident case.

"VIA FIRST CLASS MAIL

June 1, 20XX

Dr. Harry Smith
555 Treatment Drive
Pleasantville, CA 91112

Re: Lien Reduction Request

Dear Dr. Smith:

Please allow this letter to serve as a request to reduce the amount of your lien on my personal injury matter.

Throughout the course of my personal injury case, I have seen many medical providers for my treatment, for which I am grateful. I have reached a situation with the insurance company where I believe I can settle for an amount of $15,000. However, the total amount of the medical bills exceeds $10,000.

Your latest statement had an outstanding balance of $2,750. I am therefore requesting a reduction of $1,000. Please let me know if you will accept the amount of $1,750 as the full and final satisfaction of your lien on my personal injury case.

Sincerely,
Iman Pain"

Settling with lien claimants may require several communications. If they don't accept your first offer, don't be discouraged. The negotiation process is very similar to the one you are having with the other side's insurance company or the other side themselves.

Step Three: Once an Agreement is Made, Confirm It in Writing

You should confirm any agreement that you have with a lien claimant, in writing so that it is harder to dispute such an agreement when it's time to distribute the settlement check. Here is an example of a lien agreement confirmation.

"VIA FIRST CLASS MAIL

June 1, 20XX

Dr. Harry Smith
555 Treatment Drive
Pleasantville, CA 91112

Re: Lien Reduction Agreement

Dear Dr. Smith:

Please allow this letter to serve as confirmation that I have agreed to your offer to resolve my lien with your office in the amount of $2,000.

Sincerely,
Iman Pain"

Step Four: Pay the Lien Claimant

When paying the lien claimant, you should include a check and a cover letter. The check should state in the memo "Full and Final Satisfaction of [Your Name]'s Lien." Here is an example of a cover letter.

"VIA FIRST CLASS MAIL

June 1, 20XX

Dr. Harry Smith
555 Treatment Drive
Pleasantville, CA 91112

Re: Check in Full Satisfaction of Lien

Dear Dr. Smith:

   Please see the enclosed check in the amount of $2,000 made payable to Dr. Harry Smith in full and final satisfaction of your lien on my case. Thank you for your professionalism in dealing with this matter.

Sincerely,
Iman Pain
Enclosed: Check"

CHAPTER 10

How To Write A Demand Letter

At this point, your treatment is likely complete or you are approaching the statute of limitations, and you have to choose whether you're going to settle with the insurance company or other side or file a lawsuit. Now all you need is a well put together demand package to send to the insurance company or other party.

There are many different philosophies when it comes to writing demand letters. Some attorneys like to write very lengthy demand letters, which identifies a long factual and legal analysis, a long medical history with a very detailed itemized breakdown, and other portions that increase the word count.

I believe that shorter demand letters get the job done just as well. At the end of the day, regardless of the length of the demand letter, the insurance company may stall you. Additionally, the demand letter cannot generally be used as evidence because it is a confidential settlement communication. Therefore, the demand letter should be a brief and concise statement indicating the basics of the case and your demands.

The demand package comprises of two components: the demand letter, and evidence to support your claim of liability and damages.

Sample Demand Letter

For your convenience, I have included a sample demand letter that you can use in your own injury case. Please note that this demand letter is not going to work in every situation, so you will need to carefully tailor a demand letter that works for you and your specific situation. Writing demand letters is not an exact science, so it's best not to overthink them. It's more important to get the demand letter over to insurance company rather than making sure that it is absolutely perfect.

"VIA FIRST CLASS MAIL

June 1, 20XX

Adjuster
Fair Insurance Company
123 Happy Lane
Pleasantville, CA 91112

Claim #:	000456789-1
Your Insured:	Yura T. Fault
Injured:	Iman Pain
Loss Date:	June 1, 20XX

DEMAND LETTER

Dear Adjuster:

As you may be aware, I was injured with respect to the above-referenced accident. The said accident was caused when your insured was driving 15 miles above the legal speed limit, and could not stop in time before they rear-ended my car.

The liability in this case is clear. Enclosed is a copy of the police report, which states that your insured caused the collision by driving their car at an unsafe speed.

After the accident, I was transported to the hospital where I stayed overnight. I then went to an orthopedist who prescribed me with physical therapy, which I completed. My current medical bills are $12,500.

After the accident, I suffered severe pain in my neck and back, sleepless nights, and currently still have a bit of pain in my neck. My doctor says that the pain may not go away. Additionally, my doctor says that I may have to go for another round of therapy, which they say will cost approximately $5,000, and is documented in their report, which I am enclosing in this letter.

Additionally, I have been out of work for four weeks due to the injury. I make approximately $2,000 per week, as evidenced by my paystubs. Had I not been injured, I would have been able to work.

A breakdown of my damages are as follows:

1. Past Medical Bills: $12,500
2. Future Medical Bills: $5,000
3. Lost Wages: $8,000

I respectively demand that we settle this matter for $50,000. I suggest that the injury, which involved my neck, coupled with the fact that I have been out of work for a month, is more significant than a normal soft tissue injury.

I look forward to hearing from you at your earliest convenience. Thank you for your anticipated cooperation.

Sincerely,
Iman Pain
Enclosures: Traffic Collision Report, Photographs, Medical Bills, Medical Reports, Paystubs"

Parts Of The Demand Letter

1. Introduction and Liability

The demand letter consists of several parts. To begin the demand letter, the writer should be specific as to how it is delivered, the date, to whom it is addressed, and what the letter is about. For example, the person should include "VIA FIRST CLASS MAIL" or "VIA FACSIMILE." Next, regarding whom it is addressed, it should very specifically include the adjuster's or other party's name and address, skip a line, then the claim number, their insured's name, and the date of loss.

After making the proper caption, the actual letter should begin. When starting to write the body of a demand letter, a person should state who they are and how the other party caused the injury. For example, someone can say "I am John Doe and was injured as a result of your insured's negligence in the above-referenced accident. Your insured caused the accident by driving at an unsafe speed limit." Very simple and straightforward, nothing very special is needed here.

Next, a person should establish that the insurance company's insured is at fault for the accident. There are many ways to accomplish this, whether it be by a police report, witness statements, pictures, or other means. This can be done in the following way: "Liability in this case is clear as your insured was driving too fast, and the police officer put your insured at fault as per their police report." So, when including the evidence, they can also say something like, "As evidenced by the police report, the pictures of the accident, and witness statements, liability in this case is clear as your driver was clearly driving too fast and caused the accident. The police report puts your driver at fault. The witness said in the police report, 'she was driving way too fast.' The pictures also show that there are heavy skid marks leading up to my car, an indication that she had to slam on the breaks to try to avoid hitting me."

Many times, the police report will summarize the events showing who was at fault. That section can be quoted right in the demand letter. A person can say, "As stated in the police report your insured was at fault because 'they failed to yield the right-of-way,' or 'they were driving at unsafe speeds,'" or whatever the police report says.

2. Damages

The next aspect after liability is the damages portion. This is where a person is going to show what compensation they are owed and how it is calculated (excluding pain and suffering). The person can begin with a statement about their injuries, such as: "As a result of the accident, I sustained the following injuries: a sore back, whiplash, a broken finger, and any other injuries sustained."

Past Medical: You should start this section by indicating what medical treatment you have undergone as a result of the accident. You should state the types of medical providers you went to, the number of visits, and the duration for treatment. So, if you visited a general practitioner and a chiropractor several times, and your treatment lasted six months, you can say something like, "Over the last six months, I paid three visits to my general practitioner and twenty visits to the chiropractor. However, I am still in pain."

Future Medical: In the next section, talk about the future of the injury. If your injury has healed, you don't need to mention that you have recovered completely. The likelihood is that you don't know if your injury is going to manifest down the line. However, if you are going to need future medical treatment, and have some concrete evidence proving so (such as a doctor's report that says that you will need medical treatment, as well as an estimate of the treatment's cost), then you should include that in your demand letter. Otherwise, your demand for future medical treatment will not carry as much weight.

Lost Wages or Earning Capacity: If a person loses wages or the ability to earn wages due to the injury, they should include a statement regarding that loss in this section. They will want to identify the following facts:

- How long they have been out of work;
- How long they will be out of work for;
- Their wages;
- A calculation as to their past lost wages; and
- A calculation as to their future lost wages.

A statement regarding lost wages can state something like, "As a result of the injury, I was out of work for five weeks, and I make approximately $1,500 per week. Therefore, I have lost approximately $6,500 in wages."

Regarding future lost wages, or loss of earning capacity, a person may state something along the lines of, "My doctor has informed me that I will not be able to work for six months due to my injury. I made $6,000 per month, and therefore, I will lose $36,000 as a result of my injury."

Pain and Suffering: Pain and suffering is more of a discussion of facts than a discussion of damages. As discussed in the chapter "Compensation for an Injury Claim," there are many factors that encompass pain and suffering. Therefore, you should discuss the facts of your case regarding the pain and suffering that you endured. You should give a detailed report regarding your pain and suffering.

You can emphasize things that you're no longer able to do, or have had to put a temporary pause on doing because of the injury. This includes activities and hobbies, such as sports or exercising or playing musical instruments. This even includes intimacy with your spouse. So, if you are suffering from the loss of enjoyment of life, you can say something like, "Also, because of the injury, I am no longer able to exercise regularly and the intimacy with my spouse has suffered tremendously."

Emphasizing factual pain and suffering can add value to the case as they bring a claim to life. It sets you apart from being just another claim. This way, the claim gets more personal, and that is a higher risk to insurance companies since they may have more exposure if a judge or jury identifies with your case.

Breakdown of Damages: The next section that you'll want to address is the breakdown of the amount of money you claim you are owed (damages). The damages should be broken down as actual damages before giving a settlement demand. For actual damages, you should include your medical bills, lost wages, and any costs incurred as a result of the injury, and any future care you will need. Here's an example:

"A breakdown of the damages are as follows:

Physical therapy – $2500

Lost wages – $3000

Future medical care – $15,000

Total economic damages – $20,500"

Notice that there is no section that identifies the amount of pain and suffering that you are claiming. That amount will be included in your actual demand. It is not necessary to state, when writing a demand letter, exactly the amount of pain and suffering that you are claiming. This amount will be implied when you make your actual demand and the insurance adjuster should respond accordingly.

3. The Amount You Are Demanding

Next, you want to make your demand. This is the part where you actually state the monetary amount that you would like to claim. The key here is not to state the amount that you would like to settle with, because the insurance adjuster will almost always come back with a lower figure. You should start with a somewhat higher number, that way you may end up where you wanted to from the start.

Your demand should include your pain and suffering damages. Typically speaking, you can multiply your economic damages (medical bills and lost wages) by three and ask for that sum in your entire settlement demand. Pain and suffering is an abstract concept that you can argue, as discussed in the "Compensation for Your Personal Injury Claim" chapter. Therefore, if you have an economic damages claim of $20,500, you can ask for a total amount of $61,500, which includes your pain and suffering damages.

In that situation you can say something like, "I respectfully demand that this matter be settled for $61,500." Then you should qualify the demand by establishing why you are entitled to that amount. You can say something like, "Given the injury, the impact, and the fact that I'm going to need physical therapy for at least the next two years, this injury is worth more than someone who has a simple neck strain."

Policy Limits: The amount of your demand may depend on the policy limit. If the policy limit is less than or equal to the amount of the economic damages, which in the above example of $20,500, then you can make a policy limit demand. For example, if the policy limit is $15,000, you can say something like, "I respectfully demand that you tender the policy of $15,000 as a result of my injuries." If you aren't aware of the policy limit, then you can demand whatever amount you want.

You can end your letter with a response deadline and a way to contact you. You could write, "Please respond within the next two weeks, and feel free to call me at [insert phone number]." I usually follow up with the company 2-4 weeks after sending the demand.

Demand Letter to a Private Person

A demand letter to a private person is going to be a little different than one to an insurance company. Instead of asking about the insurance policy, a person can ask the other person to just pay them the amount that they are requesting. It's very important to find out whether the person has an insurance policy to cover the claim, because getting paid from an insurance company is much easier than from a private individual.

Sometimes, when dealing with a private person, it's difficult to know whether they have insurance or not. Sometimes the only way to find out is through litigation.

Here is a modified version of a demand letter to a private individual:

"VIA FIRST CLASS MAIL

June 1, 20XX

Yura T. Fault
123 Guilty Lane
Demandsville, CA 91112

Re: Accident on March 1, 20XX

DEMAND LETTER

Dear Yura T. Fault:

As you may be aware, I was injured with respect to the above-referenced accident. The said accident was caused because you were driving 15 miles above the legal speed limit and could not stop in time before you rear-ended my car.

The liability in this case is clear. Enclosed is a copy of the police report, which states that you caused the collision by driving your car at a speed that was unsafe.

After the accident, I was transported to the hospital where I stayed overnight. I then went to an orthopedist who prescribed me with physical therapy, which I completed. My current medical bills are $12,500.

After the accident, I suffered severe pain in my neck and back, sleepless nights, and still currently have a bit of pain in my neck. My doctor says that the pain may not go away. Additionally, he says that I may have to go for another round of therapy, which he says will cost approximately $5,000, and is documented in his report that I am enclosing in this letter.

Additionally, I have been out of work for four weeks due to the injury. I make approximately $2,000 per week, as evidenced by my paystubs. Had I not been injured, I would have been able to work.

A breakdown of my damages are as follows:

1. Past Medical Bills: $12,500
2. Future Medical Bills: $5,000
3. Lost Wages: $8,000

I respectively demand that we settle this matter for $50,000. I also suggest that we settle this matter at this juncture rather than taking further legal recourse.

I look forward to hearing from you at your earliest convenience. Thank you for your anticipated cooperation.

Sincerely,
Iman Pain
Enclosures: Traffic Collision Report, Photographs, Medical Bills, Medical Reports, Paystubs"

Including Bad Evidence

You may have bad evidence that could potentially hurt your claim. This would come in the form of a police report, a witness who may testify against you, an unfavorable doctor's report, or other evidence that can hurt your claim. The best thing to do in the settlement stage is to not give a lot of attention to those bits of evidence in your demand package. Your job at the settlement demand stage is to put your best foot forward. You can deal with the other side's response later.

If the other side responds indicating those negative viewpoints, and are unwilling to negotiate to a number that you can settle with, then you may have to file suit.

Here is a sample response to an adjuster who claims you are at fault because of an unfavorable police report. Keep in mind that you may need to proceed to litigation if the adjuster does not budge from putting you at fault, or if they are not offering an amount you would be satisfied with.

"VIA FIRST CLASS MAIL

June 1, 20XX

Adjuster
Fair Insurance Company
123 Happy Lane
Pleasantville, CA 91112

Claim #:   000456789-1
Your Insured: Yura T. Fault
Injured: Iman Pain
Loss Date: June 1, 20XX

Dear Adjuster:

This is in response to your last letter where you indicated that the police report states that I am at fault. The police report is inaccurate. What the other driver told the police offer is false, however the officer wrote it down in the police report as true. The police officer did not witness the accident, and their portrayal of how the accident occurred is not right.

The accident occurred as follows: [state facts different from the police report].

I hope that you give this adequate consideration when responding, and I hope that we can come to a meaningful resolution.

Sincerely,
Iman Pain"

CHAPTER 11

Negotiating A Settlement

Who is the Adjuster?

The claims adjuster is the person who is handling your claim. Many times, there will be two adjusters working on one claim, one for the property damage and the other for the bodily injury. Sometimes, the claims adjuster will refer out the claim to an attorney, so you may be speaking to an attorney about settling your claim. Even though you might think that it's going to be tougher to deal with an attorney, because they "know the law," handling the claim should be quite the opposite. They will see that it's probably more important to settle this matter rather than going to court (or at least less costly!).

The adjuster will have the most influence on how much money you will get for your settlement. So, once you settle on a number, they can send you the release agreement in order to finalize the settlement.

Negotiating the Settlement

The most important thing a person can do when negotiating a settlement is follow the three P's – preparation, patience, and persistence.

1. Preparation

To negotiate a personal injury settlement, you should be prepared to talk about your case. If the insurance adjuster is speaking with you regarding details about your case that you are unaware of, the insurance adjuster may realize that they are speaking to someone who is unprepared, and they can judge how they are going to offer to settle accordingly. So, you should be prepared in all the aspects of your case, the good facts and the bad ones too. There may be a witness whose statement is against your interests. For example, if this witness said that you're the one who's at fault, be prepared to address that topic with the insurance adjuster. If there's little property damage, but you still got injured and needed medical treatment, be prepared to speak about that as well and give reasons as to why you are injured even though there is little property damage.

Despite insurance adjusters' not being practicing attorneys, they often know more about personal injury settlements than attorneys do. Don't discount what the insurance adjuster assigned to you is saying just because they are an adjuster. They are going to have the most influence regarding how much money you're going to collect from your accident. So, you should be over prepared rather than be under prepared.

While preparing to talk about the settlement, you should go through your evidence and make sure that you know your case. If the insurance adjuster brings up something that you don't know much about, don't be alarmed. You can simply table that discussion, make a note of it after the call, and address it either in a letter to the adjuster or in a subsequent phone call.

In preparing your demand letter and demand package, you will have the opportunity to go through all your evidence (the medical bills, photographs, witness statements, and police report) so you should be pretty well prepared to take the call from an insurance adjuster, or to respond to a settlement offer with knowledge about your case.

2. Patience

Being patient during the settlement negotiation process is crucial. Irritability and anger are not going to get an insurance adjuster to write more zeros on your settlement check. When a person loses their patience, their ability to think clearly goes away, which in turn hurts the settlement process.

Additionally, the insurance adjuster may take a week or so to respond to your demand letter. If you call the adjuster repeatedly, they will sense your eagerness and insecurity about the case. This can negatively impact your negotiation.

When talking about numbers, it's important to remain very patient. Insurance adjusters will likely come back with a number that's too low for you at first. Not to worry, this happens to just about everyone. We will address this topic shortly, but the point is to not become impatient.

Something that really harms a negotiation is when a person is so impatient, they don't wait for the insurance company to make a counter offer, but instead just reduce their own offer. A person should not "bargain against themselves," but should wait for a counter offer from the other side. The insurance adjuster will likely realize how eager that person is, and they may not be willing to budge from their low offer.

3. Persistence

In addition to being prepared and patient, it's necessary to be persistent. If an insurance adjuster is giving an offer that is simply too low, you need to move forward and tell them a number that is a little higher than what you can settle with. It's important to not succumb to the mind games that the insurance adjusters play with people who are injured, such as moving very slowly with their numbers, or telling a person that their case is not worth much. They may ignore phone calls as well, or not call back for a week or so, just to drag the case along.

When responding to their offer, you should look at their number and lower yours very slowly. If you come down too fast, that can show your eagerness. Instead, be patient about lowering your offer, and go slowly. This is a settlement process. As fast as you want to get to your settlement value, it is necessary to go through the process of making the adjuster give you the number that you want.

The Offer and the Counter Offer

Before you submit your initial demand letter, you should know what your bottom line is. You should figure out what number you can settle for and walk away with. Obviously, this isn't something that you need to convey to the insurance company, but to keep at the back of your mind, so that hopefully the insurance company's offer will come in an amount equal to or higher than your bottom line. It's important not to have your first initial offer be your bottom line, because rarely is an offer made and accepted in the first try. You may be setting yourself up for failure that way.

It's important to remember not to lose your patience. Delaying is an extremely common tactic that insurance adjusters use to try and frustrate you, while saving themselves money. Their goal is to frustrate you so that you will commit to settling for a low number because you may become too impatient. In litigation, sometimes we will negotiate for *years* before arriving at the number, and sometimes we never get to a number. Sometimes a judge or jury will need to determine how much a case is worth.

When the other side comes back with their counter offer, you can come back with another counter offer that is just slightly lower than your original offer. You can repeat this process over and over until you reach a number that you can live with, while addressing each of the points that the other side brings up regarding why the case is not worth so much. Give your counter arguments as to why the case is worth more.

Repeat this process until you get to the right number, then settle the case.

It's important to note that an offer can be pulled back at any time. It's important also to know that a counter offer rejects the first one.

The Insurance Company's First Offer

By this point, you have either made an offer to the insurance company and they made a counter offer, or they made the first offer. Either way, you are probably not going to like the first number that the insurance company presents to you. You shouldn't be shocked by the low figure, and don't let it discourage you. The claims adjuster has a main goal in mind: to save their company money. The adjuster may believe that you are partially at fault, that your injuries are not serious enough, or that you're not represented by an attorney and so they don't take you seriously.

It's important to know that you aren't obliged to accept the insurance company's first offer (or any offer). Sometimes people are very impatient and just want to get that deal done, but there is usually more money than their first offer. It's a common insurance adjuster tactic to start their offer as very low. Therefore, don't be discouraged, but simply make another counter offer that a slightly below your last offer.

You should look at the insurance company's first offer as a challenge, to see how much you can get. Take the emotion out of the first offer and use it to your advantage. This is purely a business decision on the claims adjuster's part, and it should be on yours as well.

Responding to the Insurance Company's Offer

Read the insurance company's first offer carefully. It will usually have details and concerns that the adjuster has regarding your case. For example, they may state in the letter that they believe you are partially at fault. You will then need to look at the evidence and present it in a way to show that you were actually not at fault. The insurance company may have a concern about your pain and suffering, and you can reassert your position regarding those damages in a subsequent letter.

When writing your response letter, keep in mind that this is a response to the insurance company's prior letter, not a regurgitation of your initial demand letter. In your response letter, you should do the following:

- If the insurance company is the first to make an offer, your counter-offer should be the high figure you decided to start with. If you made the first offer, then the insurance company responded with their offer, you should lower your offer only slightly.

- Address the points in the insurance company's letter regarding why they believe your claim is less valuable (this will usually come in the form of any of the criticisms that they made about the claim).

Here is a sample response letter to the insurance company's offer where they denied full liability, even though the police report pins their insured at 100% fault. You will need to conform this letter to your specific factual scenario:

"VIA FIRST CLASS MAIL

June 1, 20XX

Adjuster
Fair Insurance Company
123 Happy Lane
Pleasantville, CA 91112

Claim #:	000456789-1
Your Insured:	Yura T. Fault
Injured:	Iman Pain
Loss Date:	June 1, 20XX

Re: CONFIDENTIAL SETTLEMENT DISCUSSIONS

Dear Adjuster:

Please allow this letter to serve as a response to your offer of $500.

In your letter, you write: "Due to our insured's assertion that you ran a yellow light, we must deny full responsibility and only accept 10% responsibility for this claim."

However, if you read the police report, the officer took several witness statements down and they all stated that my light was green. Additionally, the officer placed your insured entirely at fault. I do plan on calling these witnesses and the officer to testify for me should this matter proceed to litigation.

Therefore, please allow this to serve as a counter-offer to your offer of $500. I am offering to settle this claim for $10,000. This offer remains open for two weeks.

Sincerely,
Iman Pain"

Dramatize the Negotiation

You may have evidence that shows more of an emotional side to your case. These are facts that you should be referring to throughout the negotiations. This can include aspects of your case, which affect your personal life (such as the inability to do hobbies, inability to interact with your children, lack of intimacy with your spouse, etc.).

These dramatizations of the negotiation can get the insurance adjuster to raise their offer because they can realize the severity of the injuries. It also adds a personal effect to the negotiation, rather than making you just another number. This does not mean that you should get emotional about your case. It means quite the opposite, you should present facts regarding how your life is affected in a manner that raises your case's value. Here is an example:

"VIA FIRST CLASS MAIL

June 1, 20XX

Adjuster
Fair Insurance Company
123 Happy Lane
Pleasantville, CA 91112

Claim #:   000456789-1
Your Insured: Yura T. Fault
Injured: Iman Pain
Loss Date: June 1, 20XX

Re: CONFIDENTIAL SETTLEMENT DISCUSSIONS

Dear Adjuster:
    Please allow this letter to serve as a response to your offer of $500.
    I would like to add a few details to my last offer. This injury has altered several aspects of my life. Due to my broken arm, as a result of

the accident, I have not been able to play with my kids. Also, my intimate life with my spouse has suffered because of this accident. These issues cause me extraordinary emotional distress.

Therefore, please allow this to serve as a counter-offer to your offer of $500. I am offering to settle this claim for $10,000. This offer remains open for two weeks.

Sincerely,
Iman Pain"

Insurance Company Tactics

A commonly employed insurance company tactic is delaying. Insurance companies love delaying payment of claims.

If you wrote to the claims adjuster and have not heard anything for a couple weeks, then it's probably time to give them a nudge again. Two weeks is not enough time to seem eager, so go ahead and either give them a call or write them a letter asking them to respond to your last offer. If they still haven't responded, you can call and speak with their manager. If you still aren't getting a response, it may be time to file a lawsuit.

You shouldn't contact the insurance company too often. That will make you seem very eager to settle your claim and will likely reduce the amount that the claims adjuster may give you, since they believe you will just settle for any amount. Or, the adjuster can pressure you into entering into a small settlement. Quicker settlements generally result in lower settlement amounts.

Insurance adjusters are trained to look for signs that either show that a person has a weak claim or will settle for a lower value. One of those ways of showing that a person's claim will settle for a lower value is when the personal injury victim seems very eager. If you want to raise the value of your claim, remain patient.

Document the Conversations

Something that I put into practice is that after almost every conversation I document what has occurred and what's going to happen later. This is especially important when the parties are discussing settlement numbers. I would write a quick letter to the other side stating what occurred during the last conversation. Here is an example:

"VIA FIRST CLASS MAIL

June 1, 20XX

Adjuster
Fair Insurance Company
123 Happy Lane
Pleasantville, CA 91112

Claim #:   000456789-1
Your Insured: Yura T. Fault
Injured: Iman Pain
Loss Date: June 1, 20XX

Re: CONFIDENTIAL SETTLEMENT DISCUSSIONS

Dear Adjuster:
    Please allow this letter to serve as confirmation of my acceptance of your offer of $10,000 to resolve this matter. This shall also serve to confirm that you are going to send the release agreement by the end of the week. Please call with any questions.

Sincerely,
Iman Pain"

Here is an example of a letter where the adjuster made an offer, and you are simply just documenting the offer without necessarily accepting it:

Jonathan D. Roven

"VIA FIRST CLASS MAIL

June 1, 20XX

Adjuster
Fair Insurance Company
123 Happy Lane
Pleasantville, CA 91112

Claim #:   000456789-1
Your Insured: Yura T. Fault
Injured: Iman Pain
Loss Date: June 1, 20XX

Dear Adjuster:

Please allow this letter to confirm our telephonic conversation where you made a counter-offer to resolve the above-referenced accident in the amount of $5,000. This does not mean I am agreeing to the number quite yet, but I will get back to you with either an acceptance or a counter-offer shortly.

Sincerely,
Iman Pain"

Be Friendly With the Adjuster

You can attract more flies with honey than you can with vinegar. This goes a long way when trying to negotiate your personal injury settlement. It's going to be easier to settle with an adjuster whom you're getting along with, rather than one whom you're not. This is not to say that there aren't times when you have to be firm and aggressive. However, adjusters are not necessarily afraid of lawsuits, which is what most people end up threatening with. They receive those threats all day long. You can state that you intend to file a lawsuit, should the matter not be resolved, but being nasty about it may not have the effect that you want on raising the value before having to file suit.

Sometimes it is simply impossible to get along with certain insurance adjusters, especially when they are unreasonable and rude. In that situation, you could try to calm them down. However, if that doesn't work, then you may be stuck with a nasty adjuster. You can ask to speak to their supervisor if they are nearly impossible to deal with, or just file suit. Nonetheless, it's better to get along with the adjuster.

I find that in cases where I'm getting along with the insurance adjuster, settlement negotiations go a lot more smoothly.

Have Reasonable Expectations

This is a problem with a lot of people who get injured. Since they often have very high expectations, they are essentially forced into litigation because the insurance adjuster is simply not going to see eye to eye with the injured, especially if the insurance adjuster's value of the case is too far apart from the injured one's. If your medical bills are $2,000, and you have no long-term injuries, it's going to be tough convincing an insurance adjuster that you deserve $25,000 for pain and suffering. If you're having trouble figuring out how much to ask or, you can consult with a local personal injury attorney to help you get an estimate.

Quick Settlement

If the insurance adjuster is offering a quick settlement, this probably means that this is a low-ball settlement. The insurance company wants to get rid of claims as cheaply and quickly as possible, so they don't have to pay out more money. Hence, if the insurance adjuster is eager to get the money over to you, be a little suspicious. This probably means that you can get more money out of them.

Usually after a soft tissue injury car accident (soft tissue meaning you feel sore, and have no broken bones) you may not feel the effects of the injuries right after the accident. In a whiplash injury, it may take a few days for you to actually feel the injury. You may possibly be in shock and your body has not reacted to the accident. Right after your accident and when you're not feeling so injured is the perfect time that insurance companies try to take advantage of you, since you don't know how injured you are. The insurance company saves a lot of money entering into quick settlements this way.

The Insurance Adjuster is Not Your Friend

The insurance adjuster is not your friend. Their main goal is to save the company money. They are loyal to the company, not you. Therefore, always be skeptical about how much money is on the table and when the adjuster is being overly friendly. That doesn't mean that you have to act unfriendly with the adjuster, but just remember that they owe no loyalty to you.

They even may offer to meet you in person or have some friendly representative meet you in person to talk about the settlement. Don't be pressured into this. I would not recommend meeting them in person, so that you don't get talked into signing a settlement that you would not otherwise sign. The safer road is to keep everything at arm's length and deal via telephone and written correspondence.

General Medical Release

If the insurance company tries to get you to sign a general medical release, don't sign it immediately. This will essentially allow the insurance company to look up all of your medical history, and go on a "fishing expedition" to find some kind of pre-existing injury or other reasons why you were not really injured in the accident. There's no real reason to do this at the beginning stages of a negotiation. You don't want to just open up your entire private medical history to the insurance company to get your claim paid. That all eventually allows the insurance company to find any medical document in your history, even if it's not related to your injury whatsoever, and still try to use that against you.

What you can do instead is agree to a limited release to the parts of the body that were injured. If your back hurts from the accident, then you can release medical records for a certain number of years (around 5-10) in regard to any medical treatment you received for your back. If you are claiming psychological injuries, then you may want the help of an attorney before opening up any history of mental issues.

CHAPTER 12

Finalizing the Settlement

Final Steps to a Personal Injury Claim

At this point, you and the other side or adjuster have come to a number that you are both willing to settle. If you are dealing with an insurance company, then you can simply ask for them to send you a settlement agreement to review and sign. If you are dealing with a private individual, then you may need to prepare a settlement agreement for you both to sign. There is a settlement agreement at the end of this chapter which you can use.

Accepting the Settlement Offer in Writing

After a conversation with the other side or adjuster, or perhaps the adjuster sent you a letter with an offer, you should send a letter indicating that the offer has been accepted. Here is a sample letter that you can send:

"VIA FIRST CLASS MAIL

June 1, 20XX

Adjuster
Fair Insurance Company
123 Happy Lane
Pleasantville, CA 91112

Claim #:   000456789-1
Your Insured: Yura T. Fault
Injured: Iman Pain
Loss Date: June 1, 20XX

Dear Adjuster:

Please allow this letter to confirm our telephonic conversation where I accepted your offer of $6,000 to resolve this claim. Please send a settlement agreement at your earliest convenience.

Sincerely,
Iman Pain"

How Long Does the Process Take?

After you and the other side reached a number, the process should only take a few weeks until you received the settlement check. Within a week or so of accepting the offer, the insurance company should send you the settlement agreement for you to review and sign. You may want to have an attorney look over the agreement to make sure that you are signing on acceptable terms.

The Settlement Agreement

Typically, the agreement will include basic information regarding the terms of the settlement. It will include the names of the parties, the amount, and general terms.

The settlement agreement will likely include a term that once you sign the agreement, you can no longer request further payment or bring another action in court regarding the incident. Therefore, it is important for you to understand that this is likely your only opportunity for payment. Otherwise, you will have to refrain from signing the settlement agreement and you may need to pursue more aggressive courses, which are discussed later in this book.

After reviewing the settlement agreement and you find that the terms are acceptable, you can sign and return the settlement agreement and wait for your payment. Should payment not arrive within the contracted time-frame, then you may need to pursue a more serious action, such as filing a lawsuit or consulting with an attorney.

Remember to Pay Off Liens and Other Expenses

If you have liens that are on your case, such as a hospital lien or medical provider lien, you should be sure to pay them off. If they remain unpaid, then the lienholders may pursue you in court for compensation on the liens.

Sample Settlement Agreement

Here is a sample release agreement should the other side or insurance company not provide one to you. There are many ways a settlement agreement can be drafted. You may want to seek advice of a lawyer to draft the agreement according to your circumstances.

SETTLEMENT AGREEMENT

This settlement agreement is entered into this [Date], by and between the following persons and groups:

A. [Injured Person, in this case: Iman Pain]
B. [Person Who Allegedly Caused the Accident, in this case: Yura T. Fault]

WHEREAS, this agreement is in settlement of the claims and disputes involved in the incident that took place on [Date].

1. [Yura T. Fault] shall pay the total sum of $XXX by delivery to [Iman Pain], by check made payable to [Iman Pain] in exchange for a full and complete release of all claims by [Iman Pain] against [Yura T. Fault]. The monies shall be delivered to [Iman Pain] within two (2) weeks of execution of this agreement.

2. Releases. Except for the obligations/relationships recognized and/or created by this agreement, the parties release each other as set forth below from the following claims: any and all, known or unknown, anticipated or unanticipated, suspected or unsuspected, or fixed, conditional, or contingent action(s) or cause(s) of action at law or equity, suits, debts, demands, claims, contracts, covenants, liens, liabilities, losses, costs, accounts, expenses (including, without limitation, attorney's fees), and damages of every nature, kind and description arising out of, on account of, based upon, or in any way related to or arising under the events and transactions set forth herein.

3. Warranties of Parties.
   Each of the parties hereto warrants that it is the owner of the claims released herein by them, and that, as to any party other than an individual, such party is validly formed and duly existing in the state of its formation and has full power and authority to enter into and perform all the obligations contemplated by this Agreement, and that the persons executing the Agreement on its behalf are duly authorized to do so.

4. Counterparts
   This Agreement may be executed in one or more counterparts or by facsimile signature, each of which shall be deemed an original, but all of which shall constitute one and the same instrument.

5. Further Assurances.
   The parties hereto agree to execute such additional documents and perform such further acts as may be reasonable and necessary, and will otherwise cooperate fully, to effectuate the purpose of the Settlement Agreement.

6. Binding Effect.
   The provisions of the Settlement Agreement shall be binding upon and inure to the benefit of the respective parties and their

heirs, executors, administrators, agents, legal representatives and successors and assigns.

IN WITNESS WHEREOF, the parties hereto have executed this agreement on the date set forth below.

DATED:
SIGNED:
[Iman Pain]

DATED:
SIGNED:
[Yura T. Fault]

CHAPTER 13

Mediation

Another form of dispute resolution it is what's called mediation. Mediation is a nonbinding form of settlement discussions, meaning that you can go into mediation and there will not be a final decision against you or anyone. Mediation is geared towards resolving the matter without going to court or arbitration.

Dangers of Mediation

Generally speaking, mediation can be pretty helpful towards the case. Mediation can help the other side see the catering our point of view, and get them to come up with my money fairly quickly. However, mediation it can have its downsides as well.

If you choose a bad mediator, or mediator that doesn't like you or your case very much, they can try to pressure you into settling for an amount well below what you think your case is worth. This can have harmful effects on your case, because you may begin to doubt the value of your case, and the other side can start to doubt your case as well.

Choosing a Mediator

When choosing a mediator, you may want to be do a little research in regard to what kind of person the mediator is. Usually the mediator has some kind of website biography on the Internet where you can assess what kind of person the mediator is. What area did they normally practice in before becoming a mediator? Are they an attorney? Were they on the plaintiff side or the defense side? Do they have experience in cases like your accident? These are the types of questions that you may want to research before agreeing with the other side on a mediator.

Payment of the Mediator

Usually, mediation is split between the parties. Sometimes you can persuade the other side to pay for the mediator in its entirety. Insurance companies often want to avoid going to court, so sometimes they are willing to pay for mediation if they believe it will resolve the claim. If you want the other side to pay for mediation, you can tell them that you are unwilling to attend a mediation unless they pay for it in its entirety.

Mediation can run from a few hundred dollars to a few thousand dollars for half a day to a full day. Sometimes there are free mediation services. To find out, contact your local courthouse and ask for an alternative dispute resolution department or if there are free mediation services at the courthouse. You can research free mediation services online as well.

Date and Time of the Mediation

After you and the other side agree on a mediator and the mediator is contacted, they can issue a date, time and place for all the parties to meet. You should request to be seated in a separate room then the other party. That way, you can have more transparent discussions with the mediator about your case.

Arriving at the Mediation

Be sure to dress at least on the business casual side. You want to appear respectful and professional to the mediator, they can really help you with your case and help the other side see the case from your point of view to get them to come up with more money pretty quickly.

Negotiating at the Mediation

The negotiation process is somewhat different at a mediation. The mediator may try and tell you the weaknesses of your case, and try to give you a realistic spin as to what will likely happen if the case proceeds in litigation. Your job is to have a conversation with the mediator to tell them what to communicate to the other side.

When communicating your first offer, start high. The other side may start off low. Have a lot of patience when negotiating at a mediation, and move down from your number very slowly. See how much the other side is moving, and try not to move too much more than they do so that you can hit your target number at the end of the mediation process, if you reach a settlement.

Don't feel intimidated if the mediator comes down strongly against your case. You do not have to agree with anything the mediator says.

I thoroughly discuss the ins and outs of negotiating, and I recommend you read over Chapter 11, Negotiating a Settlement, prior to attending the mediation.

Unable to Reach an Agreement at Mediation

If you are unable to settle at the mediation, don't despair. Many mediations that I attend do not settle. Oftentimes, an insurance company will use mediation as a tactic to get a person's hopes up, then they won't give a reasonable offer. Mediation, if you choose to go, is just a part of the process.

You may want to ask for a range as to how much the insurance company is going to offer to you prior to attending. There is no real harm asking for this, and there is no real harm in attending the mediation.

CHAPTER 14

Small Claims Court

Small Claims Court

If your damages are $10,000 or less, and you were injured in the State of California, you may want to consider going in to small claims court. Small claims court is great, as it provides a quick way to resolve your claim.

A person may choose to submit their matter to small claims court if their case is approaching the statute of limitations, and the insurance company or the other party is not settling on an amount that the injured person would've liked. Therefore, the personal injury victim can file the lawsuit to preserve their rights and not waive the statute of limitations, then can proceed to court within a relatively short period of time.

You can sue in small claims court if you are over 18 years of age, subject to exceptions.

Lawyers are not allowed to represent people or businesses in small claims court.

Limits on Damages

California currently has a limit of $10,000 for an individual if they sue in small claims court. If a company is suing, that limit is $5,000. If the business is the sole proprietor, they can sue as an individual. You can only sue for more than $2,500 twice every year.

Deadline to File

Your deadline to file suit for your injury claim, which is discussed more thoroughly in the "Statute of Limitations" chapter is generally two years from the date of injury. There are many exceptions to this (such as if your defendant is a government entity or a medical provider). Therefore, it is very important that you go over that section to make sure you don't miss a deadline, otherwise your case will likely be barred. If you are not sure about your deadline, consult with an attorney.

Naming Your Defendant

You need to correctly name your defendant and all the defendants. The defendant is usually an individual if this is a personal injury matter. However, that individual could be in the scope and course of his employment, and therefore you should name their business as well.

In this case, you will be naming the person and/or business that hurt you, NOT their insurance company.

Filing and Serving

The first thing you need to do is obtain a claim form. This can be done by contacting your local courthouse and asking them for the form, which is required to submit a complaint for a small claims lawsuit.

After you fill out the claim form, file it with the court and pay the requisite for you. Once you have those documents, you need to have someone who is 18 years or older and not a party to the action (which means not you) serve the documents to the other party. There are professional process servers, the sheriff's department can serve, or you can have a friend serve the documents. Then they need to file what's called a "proof of service" and give that to you. The courthouse should have copies of a proof of service that can be filled out. Then you can file the proof of service at the court and get ready for your hearing.

I would recommend hiring a professional process server. That way, they should give you the proofs of service that you need, they are very familiar with the procedures, and it's less of a hassle for you than trying to get it done by a friend of yours who doesn't know how to properly fill out the proof of service.

You must comply any pre-filing and pre-serving requirements. The rules differ depending on the type of defendant you have and on the court that you are filing your lawsuit. Many courts have self-help desks for people representing themselves where you can ask questions. If you are suing the government or your lawsuit falls under a different special procedure, it is recommended that you ask an attorney for help so that the procedure is done correctly.

Getting Ready for the Hearing

Visit the chapter on "Evidentiary Hearings" to learn all about getting ready for your hearing. We did not include the hearings in this chapter since they apply to both small claims court and arbitration.

CHAPTER 15

Evidentiary Hearings

This chapter deals with small claims court hearings and arbitration hearings. This is the hearing where the judge or arbitrator is going to hear your evidence and afterward make a decision on your case as to how much money you should be awarded. There are other types of evidentiary hearings, such as the superior court trial (jury or non-jury), but conducting these trials is beyond the scope of this book. It is not recommended for a plaintiff to conduct a superior court trial by themselves. Therefore, this chapter will stick to small claims hearings and arbitration hearings.

Usual Differences Between Small Claims Court and Arbitration

Small Claims	Arbitration
Maximum a person can sue for is $10,000 (in California)	No limit
Public judge	Private judge
Cheap	May be costly
Very limited rules on discovery	Discovery is broader
Trial within weeks or months	Trial within months or years
One hearing	Many different hearings

Preparing for the Hearing

You'll want to be adequately prepared for your hearing. That means that you have all of your legal documents and evidence (see the chapter "Gathering Your Evidence" for more information).

You should consider having a trial folder, so that everything is gathered in one place. For all the pieces of evidence that you have, you should have the original and three copies. The original for the court, one for the other side, and two extra just in case someone else needs it (like a witness).

Try following these tips to increase the likelihood of success at your hearing:

1. Have all your documents and know where all of them are in organized folders.
2. Dress conservatively such as in a suit or a conservative dress; dressing appropriately shows respect for the judge or arbitrator. Dressing inappropriately may rub the judge the wrong way and could actually negatively impact the case. A man should wear a suit and tie, a woman should wear a modest dress.

If you are in small claims court, you can sit through a few court sessions to listen in on some trials. This way, you can become more comfortable as to how the small claims court is run.

The Hearing

Your hearing is likely going to be very crowded since a lot of cases get heard on the same day in small claims court. Therefore, cases are somewhat limited in time, which is why it's important that you are prepared, so you can quickly get to the heart of your matter. The arbitration hearing will likely not be crowded.

In court or arbitration, the judge or arbitrator may tell you how they want to hear your story and evidence. Follow their requests.

You should know what you are going to say in court or arbitration.

You may want to write down your statement, and practice it in front of someone close to you so that you are better prepared. Your preparation should include reviewing the following:

- Witness testimony;
- The police report, if supportive;
- Photographs of the car, accident, and injuries;
- Medical bills and records;
- Lost wages documents;
- Receipts for car damage; and
- Any other relevant documents that support your case.

1. Talk About How the Accident Happened

Wait for the judge or arbitrator to give instructions, and follow their body language. The judge or arbitrator may first want you to make a quick statement without presenting evidence, so just wait for instruction.

The first part of what you say should talk about exactly what you were doing right before the accident happened, and then how the accident occurred. For example, "I was getting off the 101 freeway and getting on the 405 freeway going south. The traffic was slowing down and the defendant rear ended me."

You should talk about how you were injured, and the fact that you were injured. For example, "I got injured when my head hit the seat. I suffered back and neck aches."

Also talk about how the defendant is liable. For example, "The defendant is liable for my injuries because they were speeding and did not look ahead to see that traffic was slowing down to get on the 405 south."

If the other person said that they were at fault, you should mention this. You should mention if they said something like, "I'm sorry," "It was my fault," or things of that nature.

If you have witnesses to the accident, ask the judge to allow them to testify at this point so that they can talk about how the other side caused the accident.

2. Talk About Your Injuries and Treatment

You should go through the evidence and explain how the accident happened, what your injuries were, how much those injuries cost you, and what treatment you'll need in the future. Talk about how long it's going to take for you to heal from these injuries as well.

Bring out every medical record and bill. Identify the treatment that you had and what the cost of that treatment was. Then say that it is the reasonable value of the treatment, because that is how much they billed and is how much you owe. If you brought a doctor or someone to testify for you regarding your injuries, medical bills, or other medical issues, you can call that person as a witness if the judge allows at that point.

When you testify regarding your own injuries, you can say something like, "On July 1, 20XX, I went to the hospital. They ran several tests. The first test was a blood test, for which they billed me $750. Then they took an X-ray, for which they billed me $2,000. Afterward, they wanted me to stay the night, for which they billed me another $2,500. In total, my medical bills were $5,250. This is the reasonable amount of the medical bills because this is how much I owe, and it is how much the hospital billed me."

You should also talk about your pain and suffering. You should mention how the accident has affected your life. Perhaps you can't play sports anymore, perhaps you can't play with your kids, perhaps you can't be intimate with your spouse. You should mention any of these things so that you give the judge or arbitrator other aspects as to how you have been affected as a result of this accident.

There are many variations of talking about your injuries and treatment. But the main point is the same: talk about all injuries, all treatments, and all bills.

3. Ask to Have Your Witnesses Testify or Try and Introduce Witness Statements

Next, you should talk about any witness statements that you have. If you brought witnesses with you, then you should tell the judge or arbitrator that you would like to call those witnesses (one at a time) to testify. The judge may ask what the witness is going to say, which you can answer. Then call each witness and have them explain what they were called for.

You may have a witness to the accident and how the other side was negligent, another witness to how the injuries affected your life, and a different witness to testify to the reasonableness of your medical bills and treatment. Call all of them, one at a time, and follow the judge's instructions on how to ask the witnesses questions or whether the judge wants to ask the witnesses what their testimony is.

4. Talk about Your Lost Wages.

Lost wages involve talking about any wages that you have lost as a result of the accident. You should offer any proof of these lost wages as well, such as paystubs, a letter from your employer, or something to prove that you have lost wages as a result of the accident. At this point, you can call a witness to testify regarding your lost wages as well.

5. Dealing with an Unfavorable Police Report

If you are in the position where you need to deal with an unfavorable police report, follow these tips. Identify all inaccuracies in the police report and say why they are inaccurate. If you have a witness who will help you prove those inaccuracies, then ask for them to testify regarding the inaccuracy of the police report as well. You can also say that the police officer had no personal knowledge of the accident since they were not there when the accident took place (only say this if they actually did not see the accident).

6. If the Defendant Doesn't Show Up

If the defendant doesn't show up, you can still present your claim. You can still get a judgment. However, you will likely have to pursue collection activities to collect the judgment.

It is possible that if the defendant gives a good reason for missing the court date (such as an emergency of some sort), then the case may be reheard at a new trial date.

7. Appealing a Small Claims Court Decision

If you are the plaintiff, you usually cannot appeal the small claims decision. That is the risk of using the quick and easy court system. However, if you were sued back by the defendant, and they win that claim, you can appeal.

When the case is appealed, the superior court doesn't consider the small claims court decision, but instead has a "trial de novo" meaning a new trial. This time, you can get a lawyer to represent you. The appeal has a specific deadline to be filed which you must follow, otherwise your appeal may be barred.

If the defendant appeals, then you will have to wait on collecting on your judgment. You will also have to bring all of your evidence and try the case again.

Collecting on a Judgment if They Don't Pay

If you're not dealing with an insurance company, but instead a private individual or small company, it may be difficult to collect on the judgment. Hence, many plaintiff's attorneys shy away from personal injury cases that do not have an insurance policy to go after. An extensive analysis of collection activities is beyond the scope of this book. However, here are some options:

- Hire a collections attorney;
- Hire a collections agency; or
- Write demand letters to the defendant for payment.

You can also check out the many books regarding collecting on a judgment. However, make sure they are California specific.

CHAPTER 16

When to Hire a Lawyer

There may be situations where you will need the help of a competent personal injury lawyer to help you with your claim. Here are some of those situations where you may be better off hiring representation.

No Settlement

Despite many talks with the other side or the insurance adjuster, you and them simply cannot see eye to eye. You can either take the next step and file a lawsuit in small claims or demand arbitration, or you can speak to an attorney to assess whether there may be another course of action that you may benefit from, such as a lawsuit filed in superior court.

The other side or the insurance company may decide that you are the one who is at fault, and they are offering no money to settle the claim. In that kind of situation, you will either need to walk away or pursue a more aggressive course of action.

Medical Expenses or Lost Wages are Too High

If your medical expenses or lost wages are getting too high, and the other side is not settling for an adequate amount, then you may want to consider hiring an attorney to help you navigate through the court system. The maximum that an individual can currently sue for in California small claims is $10,000. If your medical bills are high enough, then you may want to sue in superior court, which does not have such a limit. However, superior court cases are much more complicated than small claims cases, and therefore it would be wise to seek the help of a competent lawyer.

You Will Need a Lot of Future Medical Care

If you are going to be injured for a long time, or perhaps the remainder of your life, you should consider hiring an attorney. With these types of situations, litigating these cases can be highly complicated and expensive, as it may require the retaining and coordinating of many experts and other witnesses. Also, these types of cases are usually highly contested by insurance companies. It is likely that if you have this kind of case, you will be in litigation for a number of years as insurance companies are not easy to pay on these claims.

Medical Malpractice Lawsuits

Generally speaking, medical malpractice lawsuits are very complicated. They require the help of competent medical professionals, which are extremely costly, and they are complicated cases. It is not recommended that medical malpractice cases be litigated without the help of competent legal counsel who has experience dealing with medical malpractice claims.

Attorneys Get Better Settlements

As cynical as this sounds, it is the truth. Insurance companies and people in general take claims more seriously when there is another attorney on the end. Attorneys who have reputations for filing lawsuits and taking them through trial will likely be able to command higher settlement amounts than a person who is representing themselves.

www.ingramcontent.com/pod-product-compliance
Lightning Source LLC
Chambersburg PA
CBHW022002170526
45157CB00003B/1114